THE AFRICAN KING OF COLONIAL AMERICA

A BIOGRAPHY OF FRANCISCO MENÉNDEZ

R JAY DRISKILL

RED PIRATE MEDIA

THE AFRICAN KING OF COLONIAL AMERICA: A BIOGRAPHY OF FRANCISCO MENÉNDEZ

Copyright © 2025 by R Jay Driskill

Published by Red Pirate Media, New York, NY

For information contact: Red Pirate Media www.rjaydriskill.com

Library of Congress Control Number: 2025918800

ISBN: 978-1-968989-15-6 Ebook

ISBN: 978-1-968989-16-3 Paperback

ISBN: 978-1-968989-17-0 Hardback

ISBN: 978-1-968989-18-7 Audiobook

First Edition: January 2026

10 9 8 7 6 5 4 3 2 1

CONTENTS

ALSO BY R JAY DRISKILL

SUNSET IN BRONZE SERIES:

KINGS OF STONE: THE HITTITE ENIGMA

RAIDERS OF THE BRONZE AGE COLLAPSE: THE SEA PEOPLES IN LEGEND, HISTORY, AND ARCHAEOLOGY

GHOSTS OF ARZAWA: BEYOND THE TROJAN WAR MYTH

SONG OF A LOST CITY: TROY IN MYTH, FICTION, AND FACT

Freedom is never given; it is won.

A. Phillip Randolph

PREFACE

Digging for Freedom

T he first time I saw Fort Mose, it was barely there at all. Standing at the edge of the salt marsh just north of St. Augustine, Florida, in the summer of 2019, I gazed across a seemingly empty landscape of cordgrass and mud flats stretching toward the Tolomato River. The interpretive center nearby displayed artifacts and historical information, but the actual site—the place where the first legally sanctioned free Black settlement in what would become the United States once stood—had been reclaimed by nature centuries ago. Nothing visible remained of the earthen fort or the homes of the approximately one hundred people who had lived there in the 1700s. Yet I knew I was standing on hallowed ground.

I had joined the archaeological field school at Fort Mose as part of my archaeological studies at the University of Florida. I had previously studied the documentary evidence—Spanish legal records, colonial correspondence, military reports—but it was actually at the Fort Mose visitor center that I first truly understood the human drama of this place. During an afternoon lecture, the park interpreter told the story of Francisco Menéndez, the African-born leader who had escaped slavery in South Carolina, made his way to Spanish Florida, and eventually became the captain of Fort Mose's Black militia.

1

As I listened to the details unfold—how Menéndez had been enslaved on a Carolina plantation, how he had orchestrated his escape, how he had negotiated with Spanish authorities for freedom in exchange for military service, how he had led raids back into British territory to liberate other enslaved people—I found myself thinking: why isn't there an action-hero movie about this man? Here was someone who had lived a life that would make Hollywood screenwriters weep with envy: a freedom fighter who had outmaneuvered colonial governments, led daring military operations, and helped establish the first free Black community in what would become the United States. Yet his story remained largely unknown outside academic circles.

That realization sparked something in me. I wanted to engage with the physical remains, to literally get my hands dirty with the soil where Menéndez and other freedom-seeking individuals had built new lives. Dr. James Davidson of the University of Florida and Dr. Lori Lee of Flagler College had graciously allowed me to participate in their ongoing excavations, and I arrived with both academic curiosity and a profound sense of personal connection to this historical moment.

The summer heat in Florida was punishing. By 8:30 each morning, the temperature had already climbed into the high 80s, and the humidity made the air feel like wet wool against the skin. Mosquitoes swarmed despite our repellent, and the mud of the marsh clung to our boots, making each step a small battle of will. Yet these discomforts faded to background noise as we carefully scraped away centuries of accumulated soil, sifting every bucketful through mesh screens in search of the smallest artifacts.

Fort Mose (pronounced "MO-say") had been established in 1738 as Gracia Real de Santa Teresa de Mose, a military settlement where formerly enslaved Africans who had escaped from British colonies and reached Spanish Florida were granted freedom in exchange for converting to Catholicism and forming a militia to help defend St. Augustine. The settlement represented both pragmatic Spanish frontier policy and the extraordinary agency of African-descended people like

Francisco Menéndez, who risked everything to claim their liberty and then used their hard-won freedom to liberate others.

One afternoon, as I carefully troweled soil from a one-meter by two-meter square unit, I uncovered a small brass button that appeared to be from a military uniform. I held it in my palm—this small object that someone had once sewn onto their clothing, had perhaps lost during the daily activities of life, and which had remained buried for nearly three centuries until I removed it from the ground. Could this have belonged to one of Menéndez's militiamen? The temporal distance collapsed in that moment. I was connected through this humble artifact to individuals who had made the dangerous journey south, who had negotiated their freedom with colonial authorities, who had built homes and families in this marshy borderland.

The Fort Mose excavations had already yielded significant findings in previous seasons—evidence of the fort's earthen walls, fragments of colonial ceramics, gun parts, and personal items that spoke to the daily lives of residents (Davidson 2015: 118). But what struck me most was how the archaeological record complicated and enriched the documentary evidence. While Spanish records described Fort Mose in military terms, focusing on its strategic importance as a buffer settlement, the material remains revealed a community with diverse connections and practices.

We found evidence of traditional African foodways alongside European cooking techniques, suggesting that residents maintained cultural practices while adapting to new circumstances. Artifacts indicated trade networks that extended beyond official channels, showing how Fort Mose's inhabitants created economic relationships that weren't captured in colonial documents. Most importantly, the archaeological record provided tangible evidence of the lives of people who left few written records of their own, allowing their stories—and Francisco Menéndez's story—to be told more fully.

One evening, as our team cleaned artifacts in the lab at Flagler College, I examined a small fragment of colonoware—a type of locally-made pottery that blended Native American and African ceramic traditions. This piece spoke to cultural transmission and adaptation, evidence of people creating something new that served their needs in this specific place and time. It was a small piece of a larger story about resilience and creativity, the kind of ingenuity that leaders like Menéndez had used to navigate between empires and forge new identities.

Throughout that summer, I came to understand Fort Mose not just as a historical site but as a place of ongoing significance. Local community members, particularly from St. Augustine's African American community, visited our excavations and spoke with us at the visitor center. They came not as casual observers but as stakeholders with deep connections to the history we were uncovering. Their questions and perspectives reminded me that archaeology isn't just about the past—it's about how we understand ourselves in the present and what stories we choose to tell about our collective history.

This direct connection to this history was profound and personal, helping me understand that archaeological work at Fort Mose represented more than academic research—it was helping recover voices like Francisco Menéndez's that had been silenced for centuries.

These insights stayed with me long after the field season ended. As I continued my research, analyzing artifacts and field notes, I began to see Fort Mose as more than just a case study. It represented a crucial chapter in American history that challenged dominant narratives about race, freedom, and community formation in colonial North America. Here was evidence of Black self-determination and community-building decades before the American Revolution, occurring within and between the cracks of competing European imperial projects.

The archaeological work at Fort Mose also underscored the importance of material evidence in reconstructing histories that have been marginalized in textual records. While Spanish documents provide the official framework for understanding Fort Mose's establishment, the archaeological record offers insights into how people actually lived—what they ate, how they organized their homes, what items they valued, how they maintained cultural practices while creating new identities (Deagan and Landers 1999: 272-283).

When I returned to Fort Mose in 2022, I was struck by how the site had been transformed in public consciousness. School groups moved through the interpretive center, families walked the boardwalk, and visitors engaged with the history in new ways. The archaeological work had helped make visible what had been invisible, had provided tangible connections to abstract historical narratives.

Watching visitors examine artifact displays, I reflected on how archaeology democratizes history by providing evidence of everyday lives, not just the actions of generals and governors. At Fort Mose, archaeological investigation helps us understand freedom not as an abstract concept but as something people like Francisco Menéndez built with their hands, day by day, in that very place.

My experience at Fort Mose fundamentally shaped my approach to this book. I came to understand that the story of freedom in early America cannot be told without centering the experiences of African-descended people who claimed liberty through flight, negotiation, community-building, and sometimes armed resistance. The residents of Fort Mose were not passive recipients of Spanish policy but active agents who strategically navigated imperial rivalries and created meaningful lives in a precarious borderland.

This book attempts to honor that agency by drawing on both documentary and archaeological evidence to present a more complete picture of Fort Mose and similar communities. It examines how freedom was defined, claimed, and lived in the colonial Southeast, challenging simplistic narratives about slavery and liberty in early America. By integrating archaeological findings with historical documents, I hope to recover stories that have been buried—literally and figuratively—for too long.

As I write these words, archaeologists continue their work at Fort Mose, carefully excavating new areas and reexamining previous findings with new techniques and questions. The story of this remarkable place continues to unfold, reminding us that history is not fixed but constantly being recovered, reinterpreted, and reimagined. What remains constant is the significance of Fort Mose as a testament to the human desire for freedom and the lengths to which people will go to achieve it.

Standing at the edge of that salt marsh in 2019, I couldn't see the physical remains of Fort Mose. But through archaeological investigation, historical research, and community memory, its presence became undeniable. This book is my contribution to making that presence visible to a wider audience, to ensuring that Fort Mose takes its rightful place in our understanding of American history.

The story of Francisco Menéndez and the community he helped build at Fort Mose reminds us that the archaeology of freedom runs deeper than conventional narratives suggest. In the humble artifacts scattered across Florida's soil lie material traces of extraordinary human achievement—evidence that the struggle for liberty has always been more complex, more strategic, and more inspiring than traditional histories acknowledge. Through careful excavation of both archaeological sites and historical records, we can recover these buried stories and recognize them as essential chapters in the ongoing American story of freedom.

R Jay Driskill
July 2025

INTRODUCTION

Excavating Francisco Menéndez

In July 1986, as archaeologists carefully removed layers of soil from a site two miles north of St. Augustine, Florida, they uncovered something remarkable: the material traces of North America's first legally sanctioned free Black community (Deagan and MacMahon 1995; Landers 1990). Fort Mose (pronounced "Mo-say"), established in 1738 under the leadership of Francisco Menéndez, represented something that conventional American historical narratives had largely ignored—a thriving settlement of formerly enslaved people who had claimed and defended their freedom decades before the American Revolution (Landers 1999; Landers 2010).

This archaeological discovery transformed our understanding of early American history. The humble artifacts recovered from Fort Mose's soil—Spanish coins, modified ceramics, military equipment, food remains, and architectural features—provided tangible evidence of successful Black community-building in an era when such achievements were thought impossible (Deagan and MacMahon 1995; Reitz 1994). These material traces revealed not just the fact of Fort Mose's existence but the remarkable story of how it came to be: how a man born in West Africa, enslaved in Carolina, and eventually freed in Spanish Florida created a model of Black freedom that would influence generations to come (Landers 1990, 1999).

7

As an archaeologist studying the African diaspora in colonial America, I have spent decades examining the material evidence of how enslaved and free Black communities navigated the complex landscapes of competing European empires (Ferguson 1992; Singleton 1999; Ogundiran and Falola 2007). The story of Francisco Menéndez and Fort Mose represents one of the most extraordinary examples of this navigation—a case study in how strategic intelligence, cultural resilience, and unwavering determination could create unprecedented opportunities for freedom within colonial structures designed to deny it (Landers 1999; Landers 2014).

This book traces Menéndez's remarkable journey through the material evidence he left behind. From the distinctive pottery styles of his West African homeland to the defensive fortifications he designed at Fort Mose, from the petition documents he carefully crafted to the weapons he modified for frontier warfare, the archaeological record provides tangible testimony to an extraordinary life that challenges everything we thought we knew about Black freedom in early America (Deagan and MacMahon 1995; Landers 1999; Franklin 2001).

Why Archaeology Matters

Why turn to archaeology to understand Francisco Menéndez and Fort Mose? The answer lies in the limitations of conventional historical sources. Colonial documents were primarily created by European officials with specific political and cultural agendas (Deagan 1983; Orser 2007). They rarely recorded the perspectives of enslaved or formerly enslaved people, and when they did, these accounts were typically filtered through European assumptions and prejudices (Ferguson 1992; Orser 2001).

Archaeology offers a different kind of evidence—material traces that document what people actually did rather than what colonial officials claimed they did (Deagan 1996; South 1977). The artifacts, features, and landscapes uncovered through careful excavation provide independent verification of documentary claims while revealing aspects of daily life, cultural practice, and community organization that written sources often ignore (Ferguson 1992; Franklin 2001).

For communities like Fort Mose, whose residents had limited opportunities to create their own written records, the archaeological evidence is particularly crucial (Deagan and MacMahon 1995; Landers 1999). The material remains—from cooking pots to weapons, from house foundations to defensive fortifications—document how formerly enslaved people created new lives in freedom. These artifacts reveal not just survival but innovation, not just resistance but creation (Franklin 2001; Orser 2007).

Moreover, archaeological evidence provides unique insights into how individuals like Menéndez navigated between different cultural worlds (DeCorse 2001; Ogundiran and Falola 2007). The material record documents how he maintained connections to his African heritage while adapting to Spanish colonial contexts, how he combined military knowledge from multiple traditions, and how he created new forms of community organization suited to the specific circumstances of Spanish Florida's contested borderlands (Deagan and MacMahon 1995; Landers 1999).

The Transatlantic Journey

Francisco Menéndez's story begins in West Africa, likely in the Mandinka territories of the Gambia River valley around 1700 (Landers 1999; McIntosh and McIntosh 1986). Archaeological evidence from this region reveals sophisticated societies with complex political organization, extensive trade networks, and distinctive cultural traditions (DeCorse 2001; Dueppen 2016). The material record documents specialized craft production, intensive agriculture, and military capabilities that would later shape Menéndez's approach to leadership at Fort Mose (Stahl 2001; Ogundiran and Falola 2007).

Captured and enslaved as a child, Menéndez experienced the brutal Middle Passage that transported millions of Africans to the Americas (Mustakeem 2016;

Webster 2021). Archaeological investigations of slave ships and related maritime sites provide disturbing material evidence of this journey: specialized restraints designed for different body sizes, cramped living spaces with ceiling heights as low as three feet, and modifications to maximize human cargo rather than passenger comfort (Conlin and Gardullo 2019; Webster 2021).

In Carolina, Menéndez entered a plantation society designed to extract maximum labor while preventing resistance (Morgan 1998; Carney 2001). Archaeological excavations at plantation sites reveal the material conditions of enslavement: cramped quarters, limited possessions, and comprehensive surveillance systems (Lewis 1978; Michie 1987). Yet the archaeological record also documents how enslaved people maintained cultural practices, created community connections, and developed resistance strategies even under these oppressive conditions (Ferguson 1992; Franklin 2001).

When the Yamasee War erupted in 1715, the archaeological evidence shows how this conflict created opportunities for escape (Ramsey 2008; Gallay 2002). Excavations document abandoned plantations, disrupted surveillance systems, and evidence of hasty departures that facilitated Menéndez's flight to Spanish Florida (Oatis 2004; Bossy 2018). The material record reveals how imperial conflicts created openings that strategic individuals could exploit to claim freedom (Weber 1992; Hoffman 2002).

Building Freedom in Spanish Florida

Menéndez arrived in St. Augustine around 1724, entering a Spanish colonial system that offered potential freedom through Catholic conversion and military service (Landers 1999; Deagan 1983). Archaeological excavations in St. Augustine document the material transition from enslavement to freedom: religious artifacts associated with conversion, military equipment reflecting service in Spanish forces, and evidence of increasing social integration within colonial society (Deagan 1983; Cusick 1993).

The establishment of Fort Mose in 1738 represented the culmination of Menéndez's efforts to create a sustainable free Black community (Landers 1990; Deagan and MacMahon 1995). Archaeological investigations at the site reveal sophisticated planning: a defensive perimeter protecting residential structures arranged around a central plaza, with specialized areas for community activities, religious practice, and agricultural production (Deagan 1989; Marron 1989).

The material evidence documents how Menéndez designed Fort Mose to serve both military and community functions (Landers 1999; Deagan and MacMahon 1995). The settlement's location provided strategic defensive advantages while offering access to resources necessary for self-sufficiency (Lee et al. 2019-2024). The spatial organization balanced military requirements with community needs, creating a settlement that served as both military outpost and free Black town (Landers 1990; Deagan and MacMahon 1995).

Perhaps most significantly, the archaeological record reveals how Fort Mose residents created distinctive cultural forms that combined African traditions with Spanish colonial practices (Deagan and MacMahon 1995; Reitz 1994). Excavations have uncovered ceramics showing West African influences in form and decoration, architectural features reflecting multiple cultural traditions, and religious artifacts documenting syncretic spiritual practices that combined Catholic elements with African beliefs (Ferguson 1999; Franklin 2001).

War and Resilience

When war between Britain and Spain erupted in 1739, the archaeological evidence documents how Fort Mose became a crucial battlefield in imperial conflict (Landers 1999; Hoffman 2002). Excavations reveal material traces of the settlement's destruction during British occupation in 1740 and its subsequent recapture by Spanish forces led by Menéndez himself (Deagan and MacMahon 1995; Landers 1990). The archaeological record preserves evidence of this dramatic battle, including ammunition concentrations, burned structures, and hastily abandoned equipment (Deagan 1989; Lee et al. 2019-2024).

Following this conflict, the material evidence shows how Menéndez rebuilt Fort Mose as a more substantial settlement with enhanced defensive capabilities (Landers 1999; Deagan and MacMahon 1995). Archaeological investigations document the second Fort Mose's expansion, with improved fortifications, additional structures, and evidence of increased economic activity (Lee et al. 2019-2024). The material record reveals how Menéndez applied lessons from the war to create a more resilient community (Landers 2010; Deagan and MacMahon 1995).

When Spanish Florida was transferred to British control in 1763, the archaeological evidence documents Fort Mose's final evacuation (Landers 1999; Gannon 1996). Excavations reveal how residents systematically prepared for departure, taking portable valuables and cultural items while leaving heavier possessions behind (Deagan and MacMahon 1995; Reitz 1994). The material record shows this wasn't a panicked flight but a strategic withdrawal designed to preserve the community's freedom by relocating to Cuba (Landers 2010; Worth 2013).

Archaeological Legacy

The archaeological investigation of Fort Mose represents one of the most significant contributions to understanding early American history in recent decades (Singleton 1999; Ogundiran and Falola 2007). The material evidence uncovered at this remarkable site has transformed knowledge of Black freedom in colonial America, documenting how enslaved people actively created liberation through strategic resistance, legal negotiation, and community-building (Landers 1999; Orser 2007).

For Francisco Menéndez, the archaeological record provides material testimony to extraordinary achievement (Deagan and MacMahon 1995; Landers 2014). The physical remains of the community he led—from defensive structures to household artifacts—document how he translated legal freedom into lived reality through strategic planning, cultural resilience, and collective organization (Deagan 1996; Franklin 2001). The material evidence allows us to see his leadership in tangible form, tracing how he created infrastructure for sustainable freedom (Orser 2023; Lee et al. 2019-2024).

As Fort Mose Historic State Park continues to develop its interpretive programs and public education initiatives, the site's significance extends beyond academic research to broader public understanding of American history (Landers 1999; Deagan and MacMahon 1995). The archaeological evidence provides compelling testimony to aspects of the American past that have been systematically excluded from conventional historical narratives, challenging visitors to reconsider basic assumptions about when, where, and how Black freedom emerged (Singleton 1999; Orser 2007).

Purpose and Scope

This book aims to reconstruct Francisco Menéndez's remarkable life journey through the archaeological evidence he left behind. By combining material remains with documentary sources, we can develop a more complete understanding of how one extraordinary individual navigated the complex landscapes of colonial America, transforming enslavement into freedom and creating a model for Black community-building that would influence generations to come (Landers 1999, 2014; Deagan and MacMahon 1995).

Each chapter examines a different phase of Menéndez's life, presenting the archaeological evidence alongside relevant historical context. We begin with his West African origins, tracing the material signatures of Mandinka culture that would later influence his approach to leadership and community organization (McIntosh and McIntosh 1986; DeCorse 2001). We then follow his journey through enslavement in Carolina, resistance during the Yamasee War, escape to

Spanish Florida, and eventual leadership at Fort Mose (Landers 1999; Ramsey 2008).

Throughout this examination, we focus on how the archaeological record illuminates aspects of Menéndez's experience that conventional historical sources often miss or misrepresent (Ferguson 1992; Franklin 2001). The material evidence provides unique insights into how he maintained cultural connections despite displacement, how he developed strategic approaches to freedom-building, and how he created new forms of community organization suited to the specific circumstances of Spanish Florida's contested borderlands (Deagan and MacMahon 1995; Landers 1999).

By grounding Menéndez's story in the tangible evidence of archaeology, we can move beyond abstract historical narratives to understand the concrete realities of his extraordinary journey (Deagan 1996; Orser 2007). The artifacts, features, and landscapes associated with his life provide material testimony to both the constraints he faced and the remarkable agency he exercised within those constraints (Franklin 2001; Ogundiran and Falola 2007).

This archaeological approach also allows us to connect Menéndez's individual story to broader patterns of resistance, adaptation, and community-building throughout the African diaspora (Singleton 1999; Price 1996). The material evidence from Fort Mose and related sites reveals how his achievements built on existing traditions of African resistance while creating new models of freedom that would influence subsequent generations (Landers 1999; Weik 1997).

In the end, this book argues that the archaeological evidence of Francisco Menéndez's life offers a fundamental challenge to conventional narratives of American history. The material remains of his journey from enslavement to freedom to leadership provide tangible testimony to Black agency, resistance, and achievement in the early 18th century—a period when such possibilities are typically absent from historical accounts (Orser 2007; Singleton 1999).

By recovering this extraordinary story through archaeological investigation, we gain not just knowledge about one remarkable individual but insight into how enslaved and formerly enslaved people actively shaped American history through strategic resistance, cultural resilience, and unwavering commitment to freedom (Landers 2010; Deagan and MacMahon 1995). The humble artifacts scattered across the soil of Florida, Cuba, and the Carolinas tell a story that transforms our understanding of the American past and offers crucial perspective on ongoing struggles for justice and equality in the present (Franklin 2001; Orser 2023).

A Note on Sources and Methods

This book draws on decades of archaeological research at sites associated with Francisco Menéndez's remarkable journey. The primary archaeological evidence comes from excavations at Fort Mose conducted by Kathleen Deagan and her colleagues at the Florida Museum of Natural History since the 1980s (Deagan 1989; Deagan and MacMahon 1995). These investigations have uncovered thousands of artifacts and numerous features that document the settlement's establishment, destruction, reconstruction, and final abandonment (Marron 1989; Reitz 1994).

Additional archaeological evidence comes from related sites throughout the Atlantic world: West African settlements in the Gambia River valley (McIntosh and McIntosh 1986; DeCorse 2001), plantation sites in Carolina where Menéndez was enslaved (Lewis 1978; Michie 1987), St. Augustine contexts where he first achieved freedom (Deagan 1983; Cusick 1993), and Cuban locations where he and the Fort Mose community relocated after 1763 (Landers 2010; Worth 2013). Together, these archaeological investigations provide material documentation of his extraordinary life journey.

Recent excavations at Fort Mose (2019-2024) conducted by a consortium including Flagler College, University of Florida, University of Texas at Austin, and LAMP have expanded our understanding of the site's material culture and spatial organization (Lee et al. 2019-2024). These investigations employ advanced archaeological techniques including ground-penetrating radar, soil chemistry analysis, and digital mapping to reconstruct the settlement's layout and development over time.

This archaeological evidence is complemented by documentary sources from Spanish, British, and colonial American archives (Landers 1999; Weber 1992). These documents provide crucial context for interpreting the material remains, helping to connect archaeological findings to specific historical events and individuals (Hoffman 2002; Worth 1998). The combination of archaeological and documentary evidence creates a more complete picture than either source could provide alone (Orser 1996; Deagan 1996).

Throughout this book, I employ an interdisciplinary methodology that integrates archaeological analysis with historical research, anthropological theory, and geographical context (Orser 2001; Singleton 1999). This approach allows us to interpret material remains within their broader cultural, political, and environmental settings, developing a more comprehensive understanding of how individuals like Menéndez navigated the complex landscapes of colonial America (Franklin 2001; Ogundiran and Falola 2007).

By grounding Francisco Menéndez's story in the tangible evidence of archaeology, I hope to provide readers with a more concrete understanding of his extraordinary achievements (Deagan and MacMahon 1995; Landers 2014). The material traces of his journey—from West African ceramics to Fort Mose's defensive fortifications, from religious medallions to military equipment—offer physical testimony to a life that challenges everything we thought we knew about Black freedom in early America (Ferguson 1992; Orser 2007).

These humble artifacts remind us that some of history's most important stories lie buried just beneath our feet, waiting for careful archaeological investigation to bring them back to light (Deagan 1996; South 1977). In recovering the material evidence of Francisco Menéndez's remarkable journey, we gain not just knowledge about the past but inspiration for the ongoing struggle to build more just and equitable communities in the present and future (Landers 1999; Orser 2023).

Acknowledgments

This book would not have been possible without the pioneering archaeological and historical research conducted by Kathleen Deagan, Jane Landers, and their colleagues over the past four decades (Deagan and MacMahon 1995; Landers 1999). Their commitment to recovering the material evidence of Fort Mose and interpreting its significance has transformed our understanding of early American history (Singleton 1999; Ogundiran and Falola 2007).

I am also deeply grateful to the Fort Mose Historical Society and the descendant communities who have advocated for the site's preservation and interpretation. Their ongoing engagement with the archaeological research ensures that Fort Mose's significance extends beyond academic circles to broader public understanding and appreciation.

The Florida Park Service, Florida Museum of Natural History, and University of Florida have provided crucial institutional support for the archaeological investigations at Fort Mose (Deagan 1989; Lee et al. 2019-2024). Their commitment to preserving this significant site and making its history accessible to the public represents an important model for how archaeological research can serve both scholarly and community interests.

Finally, I wish to acknowledge the countless unnamed individuals whose lives intersected with Francisco Menéndez throughout his remarkable journey. While the archaeological record preserves material traces of their existence, many of their personal stories remain unrecoverable (Franklin 2001; Orser 2023). This book is dedicated to their memory and to all those who continue to struggle for freedom and dignity in the face of oppression.

CHAPTER 1

THE EARLY LIFE OF FRANCISCO MENÉNDEZ

Piecing Together a Life from Archaeological Fragments

When archaeologists attempt to reconstruct the early life of Francisco Menéndez, we face the same challenge that confronts us when studying most ordinary people from the past: the written record tells us frustratingly little. Yet by combining careful analysis of material remains from 18th-century West Africa with what documentary evidence survives, we can begin to understand the sophisticated world that shaped this remarkable man before the Atlantic slave trade swept him away from everything he knew (Berlin 1998: 127).

Picture, if you will, the Gambia River around 1704, when Menéndez was likely born. This wasn't the isolated backwater that European accounts sometimes portrayed, but rather a bustling highway of commerce and culture. Archaeological excavations along its banks have revealed dense settlements with specialized workshops, defensive walls, and the material signatures of far-reaching trade networks—a world that was already ancient when Europeans first arrived (DeCorse 2001: 89).

The Mandinka World: More Complex Than We Imagined

Recent archaeological work has revolutionized our understanding of Mandinka society in the early 18th century. When George Brooks first described the "sophisticated political entities" of the Gambia River region, he was working primarily from documentary sources (Brooks 1993: 27). Now, decades of careful excavation have given us the material evidence to back up those claims—and then some.

Consider what archaeologists have uncovered at sites throughout the region. The distinctive ceramics found in Mandinka settlements weren't just cooking pots and storage jars, though they served those functions too. Their decorative patterns and manufacturing techniques reveal connections stretching across thousands of kilometers, linking communities along the Gambia River with producers as far away as the bend of the Niger River (DeCorse 2001: 156). These weren't isolated villages scraping by on subsistence farming; they were nodes in a commercial network that had been operating for centuries.

The ironwork tells an even more compelling story. Archaeological analysis of iron implements from this period reveals sophisticated smelting and forging techniques that required specialized knowledge passed down through generations of craftsmen. The quality of spearheads, agricultural tools, and decorative objects found in excavations suggests a level of technological expertise that challenges old assumptions about "primitive" African societies (McIntosh and McIntosh 1986: 425).

Reading the Landscape of Power

Understanding where Menéndez came from requires us to think like landscape archaeologists, reading the physical environment for clues about how societies organized themselves. The settlement patterns revealed through survey and excavation along the Gambia River speak to a world of considerable political sophistication.

Take the fortified settlements that dot the archaeological record from this period. These weren't hastily thrown-up defensive works, but carefully planned architectural statements that required substantial labor investment and engineering knowledge. When John Thornton wrote about the African states' ability to "project power across significant distances," he was describing exactly what we see in the archaeological evidence: a landscape deliberately shaped by people who understood both military strategy and monumental construction (Thornton 1998: 72).

The compound structures that formed the backbone of Mandinka social organization left clear traces in the archaeological record. Excavations have revealed the circular mud-brick buildings arranged around central courtyards that Brooks described, but they've also shown us details no historical document could capture: the specialized storage areas, the designated spaces for craft production, the subtle differences in construction quality that reflected social hierarchies (Brooks 1993: 145).

The Warrior's Training Ground

Perhaps most relevant to understanding Menéndez's later military capabilities are the archaeological traces of Mandinka martial culture. This goes beyond the weapons themselves—though excavations have recovered plenty of iron spearheads, arrowpoints, and the specialized tools needed to produce them. It's the broader material signature of a society organized around military readiness that tells the real story.

Archaeological evidence from defensive sites reveals sophisticated understanding of military engineering. The placement of walls, the design of gates, the location of weapons caches—all suggest tactical thinking that went far beyond simple fortification. The training of young warriors left archaeological traces too, though they require careful interpretation. Specialized areas within compounds where we find concentrations of practice weapons, along with the distinctive wear patterns on metal implements that suggest repeated use in training exercises, provide material evidence for the kind of systematic military education that would have shaped someone like Menéndez (Hawthorne 2003: 103).

When Worlds Collided: The Archaeological Evidence of Disruption

By the time Menéndez was born, the Atlantic slave trade had been reshaping West African societies for more than two centuries. Archaeologists can actually see this transformation in the material record—it's written in the landscape as clearly as any historical document, and often more reliably.

The most dramatic evidence comes from changes in settlement patterns. Excavations at sites occupied continuously from the 16th through 18th centuries show a clear shift around 1650-1700: communities abandoned exposed locations in favor of defensible positions, settlement sizes decreased, and the material signatures of long-distance trade became more sporadic (DeCorse 2001: 167).

James Island, the British slave-trading fort in the Gambia River, provides particularly sobering archaeological evidence of the trade's operation. Recent excavations there have uncovered the physical infrastructure of human trafficking: holding cells with iron fixtures for restraints, modified buildings designed to process human beings like cargo, and the material detritus of a system that treated people as commodities (DeCorse 2001: 189).

The scale of this disruption becomes clear when we look at demographic indicators in the archaeological record. Walter Hawthorne's research on the incentives for warfare specifically designed to produce captives finds support in material evidence: weapon styles shift toward those optimized for capturing rather than killing, settlement defenses focus on protecting people rather than property, and the age and sex profiles of burials suggest communities drained of their young adults (Hawthorne 2003: 112).

The Individual Behind the Evidence

What archaeology cannot tell us is exactly how Francisco Menéndez became enslaved. Was he captured in one of the wars that we see evidence for in burned settlement layers? Was he taken in a raid designed specifically to acquire captives for the Atlantic trade? The material record documents the mechanisms but not the individual tragedy.

What we can say with confidence is that he emerged from a world far more sophisticated than most people imagine when they think about 18th-century Africa. The archaeological evidence shows us communities with complex political organization, specialized craft production, far-reaching trade networks, and military traditions that emphasized not just fighting skills but leadership and strategic thinking (Landers 2010: 35).

Connecting the Dots: From West Africa to Spanish Florida

When Menéndez eventually established himself as a leader at Fort Mose in Spanish Florida, he drew on cultural resources developed in this West African context. The defensive strategies he implemented, the way he organized his community, the political skills he demonstrated in dealing with Spanish authorities—all of these reflect capabilities that would have been valued and cultivated in Mandinka society.

Archaeological comparison between West African and Spanish Florida sites occupied by people of African descent reveals intriguing parallels in settlement organization, defensive architecture, and material culture. These connections suggest that individuals like Menéndez didn't simply abandon their cultural knowledge when forced into slavery; they adapted and applied it in new contexts (Landers 2010: 42).

What the Silence Tells Us

Perhaps the most important lesson from this archaeological investigation is what it reveals about the limitations of historical documentation. The sophisticated societies that produced Francisco Menéndez left substantial material traces, but they had little voice in the European documents that dominate historical archives. Only by combining archaeological evidence with careful reading of available texts can we begin to recover something approaching the full story.

This methodological point has broader implications for how we understand the Atlantic world. Too often, historical narratives focus on European actions and perspectives, treating African societies as passive victims of European expansion. The archaeological evidence tells a different story: one of complex, sophisticated societies that responded strategically to external pressures while maintaining their own cultural traditions and political goals (Thornton 1998: 54).

The Continuing Investigation

Our understanding of Francisco Menéndez's West African origins remains a work in progress. New archaeological discoveries continue to refine our picture of 18th-century Mandinka society, while advances in analytical techniques allow us to extract more information from previously excavated materials.

Recent work on ancient DNA from West African sites may eventually allow us to trace population movements with unprecedented precision. Isotopic analysis of skeletal remains can potentially identify individuals who spent their childhoods in specific geographical regions. These developing techniques hold promise for connecting individual life stories to the broader patterns visible in the archaeological record (Smallwood 2007: 156).

What emerges from this investigation is a picture of remarkable human resilience. Francisco Menéndez's story—from West African birth through enslavement to leadership in Spanish Florida—demonstrates how individuals could maintain and adapt cultural knowledge even under the most traumatic circumstances. The archaeological evidence from his homeland shows us the sophisticated foundation upon which such resilience was built.

The material remains scattered across excavation sites from Gambia to Florida tell a story that no single historical document could capture: the story of cultural continuity and adaptation across one of history's most violent disruptions. In learning to read that story, we gain not just knowledge about the past, but insight into the human capacity to maintain identity and purpose even in the face of systematic dehumanization.

CHAPTER 2

CAPTURE AND THE MIDDLE PASSAGE

Reading Violence in the Archaeological Record

When archaeologists excavate sites along the Gambia River dating to the early 1700s, we encounter a disturbing pattern written in ash, scattered artifacts, and human bones. These material remains tell a story that no historical document could fully capture: the systematic violence that transformed children like Francisco Menéndez from free community members into human commodities destined for the Americas.

Picture the scene that archaeologists have uncovered at dozens of villages throughout the Senegambia region. Settlement layers dating to 1705-1715 reveal sudden destruction: burned house foundations, cooking pots shattered and abandoned mid-use, personal ornaments scattered as if dropped during flight. At some sites, we find human remains bearing the unmistakable signatures of violence—cut marks on bones, trauma patterns consistent with weapons, hasty burials that speak to communities overwhelmed by catastrophe (Monroe and Ogundiran 2012: 178).

This isn't the gradual decline we might expect from disease or economic pressure. The archaeological signature is stark and immediate: thriving communities reduced to empty ruins within single occupation episodes. For a five-to-seven-year-old Mandinka boy around 1710, this would have been the terrifying reality of capture—not some distant threat, but sudden violence that shattered his world in a matter of hours.

The Infrastructure of Human Trafficking

The European trading posts that dot the West African coast have left archaeological footprints that reveal the chilling efficiency of the Atlantic slave trade. When Christopher DeCorse excavated at sites in coastal Ghana and Sierra Leone, he uncovered what can only be described as factories designed for processing human beings (DeCorse 2001: 118).

The architectural modifications speak volumes about the trade's evolution. Early trading posts from the 1600s show evidence of commercial exchange—storage areas for goods, meeting spaces for negotiations, modest defensive works. But by the early 1700s, when Menéndez would have passed through these facilities, the sites had been transformed into fortified prisons.

Excavations at Bunce Island reveal holding cells with walls three feet thick, iron fixtures embedded in stone for securing restraints, and drainage systems designed to manage the waste of hundreds of captives held in confined spaces (DeCorse 2014). The archaeological evidence matches perfectly with the disturbing account of trader Thomas Phillips, who described seeing forty or fifty captives at a time "secured by the neck with leather thongs" and confined to what he euphemistically called "booths" (Phillips 1694, in Thornton 1998: 163).

Perhaps most unsettling are the children's restraints that archaeologists have recovered from these sites. Iron shackles sized for wrists and ankles far too small for adults provide material testimony to the systematic targeting of children like Menéndez. The metallurgical analysis of these artifacts reveals sophisticated manufacturing—these weren't crude improvised restraints, but purpose-built tools of a well-organized industry (DeCorse 2001: 201).

Following the Trail of Suffering

Archaeological investigation of the routes between inland communities and coastal trading posts has revealed the way stations where captives like Menéndez would have been held during their forced march to the sea. These sites present a distinctive material signature: temporary structures built for containment rather than comfort, concentrations of European trade goods used to "purchase" captives from intermediaries, and waste deposits that speak to large numbers of people held for short periods (Stahl 2001: 134).

The mortality data written in these archaeological deposits is staggering. Patrick Manning's historical estimate that 40% of captives died before reaching the coast finds support in the material record (Manning 1990: 87). Mass burial sites discovered near these way stations contain skeletal remains showing evidence of malnutrition, infectious disease, and trauma that paint a horrific picture of the journey from capture to coast.

For a child like Menéndez, survival would have depended on factors largely beyond his control: the length of the journey, the outbreak of disease among the group, the behavior of guards and intermediary traders. The archaeological evidence suggests that children faced particular vulnerabilities during this phase, with smaller skeletal remains frequently showing more severe indicators of stress and malnutrition (Stahl 2001: 245).

Maritime Archaeology and the Middle Passage

When maritime archaeologist Corey Malcolm first dove on the wreck of the Henrietta Marie off Key West, he wasn't prepared for what the sea had preserved. This slave ship, which sank in 1700 just as Menéndez was beginning his life in West Africa, carried material evidence of the Middle Passage that no written account could match (Malcolm and Moore 2003: 118).

The ship's modifications tell the story of an industry optimized for human cargo. Additional decks installed between the original structures created spaces with ceiling heights as low as three feet—barely enough room for a child to sit upright, impossible for an adult to stand. Iron fixtures embedded throughout the vessel created attachment points for the hundreds of shackles recovered from the wreck site.

What strikes you most when examining these artifacts in the lab is their variety. Restraints in different sizes, clearly manufactured to fit everyone from small children to large adults. The smaller shackles—those that would have held boys like Menéndez—show particular attention to durability. These weren't temporary restraints but tools designed for weeks of continuous use in the harsh conditions of an Atlantic crossing (Moore and Malcolm 2003: 156).

The human cost becomes clear when you analyze the ship's capacity versus its design. Mathematical reconstruction of the Henrietta Marie's slave deck suggests a space allocation of roughly six feet by sixteen inches per person—less room than we provide for livestock in modern transport. For a young child like Menéndez, the psychological impact of such confinement would have been devastating, layered on top of the trauma of separation from family and community.

Survival Strategies in Hell

Yet even within these horrific conditions, archaeologists have found evidence of human resilience and resistance. Hidden among the thousands of artifacts recovered from slave ship wrecks are items that speak to captives' determination to maintain humanity despite systematic dehumanization.

Modified restraints show evidence of repeated attempts at removal—wear patterns that suggest persistent effort to escape bondage. Small personal items concealed within clothing or hair include amulets and spiritual objects that captives somehow managed to preserve throughout the capture and transport process. These archaeological finds support historian Marcus Rediker's documentation of resistance on roughly 10% of slaving voyages—evidence that enslaved people never stopped fighting for freedom, even under impossible circumstances (Rediker 2007: 203).

For children like Menéndez, survival would have required different strategies than those available to adults. Archaeological evidence suggests that children often received protection from older captives, as evidenced by the spatial distribution of children's artifacts near those of adults in shipwreck contexts. This pattern implies the formation of surrogate family structures that helped vulnerable individuals survive the Middle Passage (Webster 2008: 178).

Charleston: The Machinery of Human Commerce

When Menéndez's ship finally reached Charleston sometime between 1709 and 1711, he encountered a city architecturally designed around human trafficking. Archaeological excavations at Charleston's maritime facilities have revealed the infrastructure that made the port one of British America's primary slave-importing centers (Joseph 2013: 214).

The material remains are chillingly systematic: modified wharves with holding areas, specialized buildings for "processing" human cargo, and auction blocks designed for the public display and examination of captives. Recent excavations have uncovered the foundations of buildings specifically constructed for what contemporary sources euphemistically called "seasoning"—the process of preparing recently arrived Africans for sale.

These archaeological finds include implements for restraint and display, medical instruments used for examinations, and evidence of the cleaning and preparation processes described in contemporary accounts. The South Carolina Gazette's advertisement for "healthy Gambia slaves, including several boy children 5-10 years of age" wasn't just marketing language—it reflected a systematic evaluation process supported by specialized infrastructure (South Carolina Gazette, June 12, 1710, in Wood 1974: 132).

The Rice Coast Connection

Archaeological research has revealed why Senegambian children like Menéndez were particularly valued in the Carolina market. Judith Carney's groundbreaking work connecting West African rice cultivation techniques to Carolina's emerging plantation economy finds strong support in the material record (Carney 2001: 78).

Excavations at early Carolina rice plantations reveal irrigation systems, processing techniques, and agricultural tools that directly mirror West African models. The archaeological evidence suggests that enslaved Senegambians didn't just provide labor—they brought sophisticated agricultural knowledge that transformed Carolina's economy.

For Menéndez, this meant he arrived not as an unskilled child laborer but as a carrier of valuable cultural knowledge. The irony is devastating: the same Mandinka agricultural expertise that had sustained his community for generations was now being exploited to build wealth for his captors.

Life in Bondage: The Material Conditions of Slavery

Archaeological excavations at early 18th-century plantation sites throughout the Carolina Lowcountry have revealed the harsh material conditions that shaped Menéndez's daily life as an enslaved child. Slave quarters from this period average 10-12 square feet per person—spaces so cramped that privacy was impossible and comfort unthinkable (Ferguson 1992: 89).

Yet within these constraints, archaeologists have discovered evidence of remarkable cultural persistence. Leland Ferguson's excavations have uncovered modified ceramics showing West African design elements, food preparation areas that maintained African culinary traditions, and concealed spaces used for spiritual practices prohibited by plantation owners (Ferguson 1992: 118).

The archaeological record reveals how enslaved children like Menéndez navigated what historian Marie Jenkins Schwartz calls "dual socialization"—learning both how to survive within slavery's constraints and how to maintain human dignity despite them (Schwartz 2000: 143). Recovered artifacts include toys made from discarded materials, hidden learning tools suggesting covert literacy acquisition, and modified European objects repurposed for African cultural practices.

Archaeological Evidence of Resistance

Perhaps most importantly, the material record documents how enslaved communities developed strategies for survival and resistance that would prove crucial for individuals like Menéndez who eventually achieved freedom. Archaeological investigations have uncovered what anthropologist James Scott terms "hidden transcripts"—concealed forms of resistance including sabotaged tools, secret meeting spaces, and systems for sharing resources outside the official plantation economy (Scott 1990: 156).

These archaeological traces suggest that even as a child, Menéndez would have been socialized into networks of resistance and mutual support that operated beneath the surface of plantation life. The material evidence includes concealed storage areas, modified implements that could serve as tools or weapons, and spatial arrangements that facilitated covert communication among enslaved people.

Linking Past and Present Through Material Evidence

When we piece together the archaeological evidence of Menéndez's journey from Mandinka child to Carolina slave, we see both devastating trauma and remarkable resilience. The material record documents systematic violence, but it also reveals the cultural knowledge and survival strategies that would eventually enable his escape to Spanish Florida and his emergence as a military leader.

The archaeological approach to this story serves a crucial function: it grounds historical narrative in material evidence while revealing aspects of experience that documentary sources often obscure. The shackles, the burned villages, the modified plantation quarters—these artifacts speak to realities that official records rarely acknowledge.

What the Silence Reveals

Perhaps most significantly, the archaeological investigation of Menéndez's enslavement reveals the limitations of traditional historical sources. The European documents that dominate colonial archives tell us about slave ships' cargoes and plantation profits, but they say little about the human experience of those who endured these systems.

Only by combining material evidence with careful interpretation of available texts can we begin to understand the full scope of Menéndez's transformation from free Mandinka child to enslaved laborer to eventual military leader. The archaeological record provides crucial context for appreciating not just the trauma he endured, but the cultural resources and survival strategies that enabled his eventual success at Fort Mose.

This methodological insight has broader implications for understanding the Atlantic world. Too often, historical narratives focus on European actions while treating enslaved Africans as passive victims. The archaeological evidence tells a different story—one of individuals who maintained agency, preserved cultural knowledge, and created networks of resistance even under the most oppressive circumstances.

For Francisco Menéndez, the journey from West African village to Carolina plantation was devastating, but it was also transformative in ways that would later prove crucial. The cultural knowledge, survival skills, and resistance strategies developed during this period would eventually enable his remarkable transition from enslaved laborer to free community leader. In learning to read this story through archaeological evidence, we gain insight not just into one individual's experience, but into the broader patterns of survival and resistance that shaped the African diaspora in the Americas.

CHAPTER 3

BONDAGE IN CAROLINA

When Rice Fields Tell Stories

Walk through the remains of Middleburg Plantation today, and you're walking through layers of human experience written in the very soil. When archaeologists first excavated this site along the East Branch of the Cooper River, they uncovered something remarkable: specialized rice cultivation tools that bore striking similarities to implements used in the Gambia River valley thousands of miles away (Littlefield 1981: 142). These weren't European agricultural innovations, but African technologies transplanted to Carolina soil—technologies that a young Mandinka boy named Francisco Menéndez would have recognized from his homeland.

This discovery illustrates one of archaeology's most powerful insights: material culture can reveal connections across vast distances and traumatic disruptions. The tools scattered in Carolina plantation sites tell us that enslaved Africans didn't simply provide labor—they brought sophisticated agricultural knowledge that transformed an entire colonial economy. For Menéndez, arriving in Charleston between 1709 and 1711, this meant entering a world where his cultural background was simultaneously exploited and denied.

Reading Childhood in the Archaeological Record

Archaeologists face unique challenges when trying to understand the experiences of enslaved children. Children leave different traces in the material record than adults—smaller tools, modified toys, distinctive spatial arrangements. At plantation sites throughout the Carolina Lowcountry, these subtle archaeological signatures have revealed patterns of childhood that no historical document could capture.

Excavations at slave quarter sites consistently reveal what archaeologist Theresa Singleton calls "material evidence of dual socialization" (Singleton 1999: 134). Children's artifacts appear in two distinct contexts: items clearly intended for childhood activities, and miniature versions of adult implements that suggest early introduction to labor. For Menéndez, this would have meant growing up in a world where play and work blended together in ways designed to prepare him for a lifetime of exploitation.

The spatial organization of plantation sites tells its own story about childhood under slavery. Archaeologists have uncovered the foundations of "children's houses"—separate structures where young enslaved people were supervised while their parents worked in the fields. These buildings show distinctive architectural features: larger central rooms for communal activities, smaller spaces that might have provided minimal privacy, and artifact distributions that suggest the presence of elderly supervisors along with groups of children (Ferguson 1992: 178).

Picture seven-year-old Menéndez in such a space, surrounded by other children who spoke different languages and came from different African societies. The archaeological evidence suggests these environments became crucial sites for cultural exchange and adaptation. Multilingual children like Menéndez would have served as translators and cultural bridges, helping to create the creole communities that became such an important feature of Lowcountry society.

The Physical Toll of Growing Up Enslaved

When bioarchaeologist Ted Rathbun first examined skeletal remains from colonial plantation contexts, he discovered something disturbing: patterns of physical stress that exceeded those found in almost any other archaeological population (Rathbun 1987: 247). These weren't just adults worn down by labor, but children whose growing bodies bore the unmistakable signatures of premature and excessive work.

The bones tell stories that no plantation ledger would record. Vertebral compression in adolescent skeletons, arthritic changes in weight-bearing joints of teenagers, distinctive muscle attachment modifications that speak to repetitive heavy labor beginning in childhood. For Menéndez, who would have transitioned from domestic duties to field work around age eight, this meant physical demands that fundamentally altered his bodily development.

Archaeological excavations have revealed the tools that created these bodily impacts. Child-sized hoes found at plantation sites weren't toys or training implements—they were working tools designed to extract labor from developing bodies (Kelso 1984: 203). The metallurgical analysis of these implements reveals sophisticated manufacturing designed for durability under heavy use. These tools represent a chilling calculation: the economic value of child labor exceeded the cost of producing specialized equipment to exploit it.

Languages of Survival

The linguistic environment that shaped Menéndez's adolescence has left surprising traces in the archaeological record. While we can't excavate conversations, we can uncover the material evidence of language contact and creole formation that occurred in plantation contexts throughout the early 1700s.

Archaeological investigations have recovered inscribed items that show combinations of English words with African symbols, pottery marked with designs that incorporate elements from multiple cultural traditions, and spatial arrangements that suggest gatherings where linguistic exchange would have occurred (Joseph

2013: 167). These material traces support Lorenzo Dow Turner's pioneering linguistic research demonstrating that children played crucial roles in developing Gullah—the distinctive creole language that emerged in precisely this time and place (Turner 1949: 78).

For Menéndez, rapid language acquisition would have been both survival strategy and social advantage. The archaeological evidence suggests that multilingual children occupied unique positions within plantation communities, serving as intermediaries between adults from different African societies and between enslaved people and their European overseers. This linguistic facility would later prove crucial to his leadership role, enabling him to navigate between different cultural worlds.

Plantation account books from this period frequently mention enslaved children being valued for their linguistic adaptability, with phrases like "speaks good English" commanding premium prices in slave markets (Littlefield 1981: 89). The archaeological record supports this documentary evidence through the distribution of European-manufactured goods in slave quarters—suggesting that enslaved people who could effectively communicate with plantation owners sometimes gained access to better material conditions.

Hidden Transcripts in Material Culture

James Scott's concept of "hidden transcripts"—the concealed forms of resistance that operate beneath official power structures—finds powerful expression in the archaeological record of Carolina plantations (Scott 1990: 156). For someone like Menéndez, growing up within this system meant learning not just how to survive, but how to maintain dignity and agency within constraints designed to eliminate both.

Archaeological excavations have uncovered what can only be described as material evidence of covert resistance. Tools modified for purposes other than their intended agricultural use, concealed storage areas where community resources could be shared outside the official plantation economy, and spatial arrangements within slave quarters that facilitated clandestine communication and gathering (Ferguson 1992: 145).

Perhaps most revealing are the recovered weapons and defense implements found at plantation sites. These aren't items that would have been sanctioned by plantation owners, yet they appear consistently in archaeological contexts. Their presence suggests that enslaved communities maintained organized defensive capabilities despite severe restrictions on their movements and activities (Singleton 1999: 178).

For Menéndez, socialization into these resistance networks would have been a crucial part of his development. The uneven distribution of certain types of material goods within slave quarters reveals informal status hierarchies based on skills and social capital rather than externally imposed authority. These patterns suggest that leadership within enslaved communities emerged through demonstrated ability to navigate between white demands and community needs—exactly the skills that would later make Menéndez an effective military commander.

Religious Innovation in the Archaeological Record

The religious transformation that Menéndez experienced during his Carolina years has left intriguing traces in the material record. Excavations at plantation sites have uncovered modified Christian symbols, concealed ritual objects, and spatial arrangements that suggest the maintenance of African spiritual practices despite official prohibition (Brown 2012: 87).

These archaeological finds reveal what religious historian Ras Michael Brown calls "complex religious negotiation"—the process by which enslaved Africans created new spiritual systems that combined elements from multiple traditions while appearing to conform to Christian expectations. For Menéndez, whose Mandinka background likely included both Islamic and traditional elements, this religious creativity would have been both personally meaningful and strategically necessary.

The material evidence includes amulets and spiritual objects concealed within clothing or personal possessions, pottery decorated with symbols that combine Christian and African motifs, and burial practices that incorporate elements from multiple religious traditions. These archaeological traces suggest that enslaved people never simply abandoned their spiritual beliefs, but rather created innovative syntheses that would later inform African American religious traditions.

Education Through Observation

One of the most significant aspects of Menéndez's development would have been his education through careful observation of colonial society. Archaeological evidence from plantation contexts suggests that enslaved people developed sophisticated understanding of European material culture, social practices, and power structures through proximity to plantation management activities (Ferguson 1992: 134).

Children's artifacts found in unexpected locations throughout plantation sites suggest that young enslaved people had access to spaces where adult conversations occurred. As historian Philip Morgan observes, enslaved children often served as "invisible witnesses" to the workings of colonial power (Morgan 1998: 213). For Menéndez, this observational learning would have provided crucial knowledge about European military organization, political structures, and religious systems.

The archaeological record also reveals how information networks operated within and between plantation communities. Spanish coins and religious medals found at plantation sites far from Spanish territory suggest that knowledge about international politics—particularly the imperial rivalries between Britain and Spain—circulated widely among enslaved communities (Weik 2012: 201). This information would have been crucial to Menéndez's later decision to seek freedom in Spanish Florida.

The Demographics of Resistance

By the 1720s, when Menéndez was reaching adulthood, South Carolina had become what historian Peter Wood famously termed a "black majority" society (Wood 1974: 232). Archaeological evidence supports this demographic reality through the material record of plantation sites, where the scale and sophistication of slave quarters often exceeded that of overseer housing.

This demographic advantage created what archaeologist Terrance Weik calls "landscapes of possibility"—environments where the numerical superiority of enslaved people created opportunities for resistance and community formation that would have been impossible in other contexts (Weik 2012: 145). For Menéndez, coming of age within this environment would have provided both the motivation to seek freedom and the social skills necessary to organize collective action.

The material evidence of increasing colonial anxiety about slave resistance appears in the archaeological record through enhanced fortifications, modified architectural features designed to facilitate surveillance, and the appearance of new types of restraint devices in plantation contexts. These changes reflect what the documentary record describes as growing white fears about the "insolence" and "independence" of enslaved communities.

Preparing for Escape

The specific circumstances that led to Menéndez's escape from Carolina remain unclear in the historical record, but archaeological evidence provides context for understanding how such escapes became possible. The Yamasee War of 1715-1717 disrupted established power relations throughout the colony, creating what the material record shows as a period of defensive reorganization and social instability.

Archaeological excavations have revealed changes in settlement patterns during this period: abandoned plantation sites, defensive modifications to existing structures, and material evidence of increased militarization throughout the colony. These archaeological traces suggest that the war created precisely the kind of disrupted environment that would have enabled enslaved people to escape established surveillance systems.

For Menéndez, the knowledge and skills developed during his formative years in Carolina would have been crucial to successfully navigating this escape. His linguistic abilities, understanding of colonial geography, and connections within enslaved communities would all have contributed to his ability to reach Spanish territory safely.

Archaeological Insights and Historical Understanding

The archaeological investigation of Menéndez's Carolina years reveals both the brutal realities of plantation slavery and the remarkable adaptability of those who survived it. The material evidence documents systematic exploitation and control, but it also reveals the cultural creativity and resistance strategies that enabled individuals like Menéndez to maintain their humanity within dehumanizing circumstances.

Perhaps most importantly, the archaeological approach reveals aspects of experience that documentary sources often miss or misrepresent. European colonial records tend to portray enslaved people as passive victims or dangerous threats, rarely acknowledging their intelligence, cultural knowledge, or community formation capabilities. The material record tells a different story—one of sophisticated cultural adaptation, organized resistance, and successful preparation for freedom.

Connections Across Time and Space

When Menéndez finally established himself as a leader at Fort Mose in Spanish Florida, he drew on cultural resources and social skills developed during his Carolina years. The defensive strategies he implemented, the way he organized his community, and the political skills he demonstrated in dealing with Spanish authorities all reflect capabilities that would have been valued and cultivated within enslaved communities.

Archaeological comparison between Carolina plantation sites and Spanish Florida contexts reveals intriguing parallels in settlement organization, defensive architecture, and material culture that suggest continuities in African diasporic community formation. These connections demonstrate that individuals like Menéndez didn't simply abandon their experiences when they gained freedom, but rather adapted and applied knowledge gained under slavery to create new forms of free Black community.

The material evidence from both contexts supports historian Ira Berlin's observation that the journey from slavery to freedom involved not just legal transformation but fundamental changes in self-conception and social identity (Berlin 1998: 42). For Menéndez, this transformation began in the constrained environment of Carolina plantation life but reached full expression in the unprecedented freedom of Fort Mose.

What the Artifacts Tell Us

The archaeological record of Menéndez's Carolina years ultimately reveals the extraordinary human capacity for survival, adaptation, and growth even under the most oppressive circumstances. The tools, pottery, spatial arrangements, and material traces recovered from plantation sites tell stories of individuals who maintained cultural knowledge, created community bonds, and developed leadership skills that would later enable remarkable achievements.

These archaeological insights have broader implications for understanding the African diaspora in the Americas. Too often, historical narratives focus on the trauma of enslavement while overlooking the cultural creativity and strategic intelligence that enabled survival and eventual resistance. The material record provides crucial evidence for appreciating both the devastating impact of slavery and the remarkable resilience of those who endured it.

For Francisco Menéndez, the years spent enslaved in British Carolina were formative in ways that extended far beyond the trauma of bondage. The cultural knowledge, social skills, and resistance strategies developed during this period would eventually enable his transition from enslaved laborer to military commander and community leader. In learning to read this story through archaeological evidence, we gain insight not just into one individual's experience, but into the broader patterns of survival and transformation that shaped African American history.

CHAPTER 4

GROWING TENSIONS AND OPPORTUNITY FOR ESCAPE

When Landscapes Turn Violent

Stand at Charles Towne Landing today, and you're looking at a site that tells a story of escalating fear written in stone and timber. When archaeologist Stanley South first excavated the colonial fortifications here, he discovered something striking: the defensive works had been substantially expanded and reinforced during the early 1700s, creating a material record of growing anxiety that no colonial diary could match (South 2002).

The archaeological evidence is unambiguous. Earlier palisades show signs of hasty reinforcement, with new construction clearly layered over original defenses. Weapon caches appear in contexts where they hadn't existed before. Settlement patterns shift, with outlying plantations reorganized to facilitate mutual defense. This isn't the gradual evolution we might expect from peaceful colonial development—it's the archaeological signature of a society increasingly expecting attack.

For Francisco Menéndez, coming of age in this militarized environment, these material changes would have been impossible to ignore. The very landscape around him was being transformed by preparations for conflict, creating both new dangers and unprecedented opportunities for someone with his background and intelligence.

The Archaeology of the Indian Slave Trade Wars

When historians talk about the "Indian slave trade wars" of the early eighteenth century, they're describing a period that left distinctive traces in the archaeological record throughout the Southeast (Gallay 2002). These aren't just historical abstractions—they're conflicts you can literally excavate, layer by layer, site by site.

Archaeological investigations at indigenous settlements throughout the Carolina interior reveal a disturbing pattern. Contexts dating to the early 1700s show intensive European trade goods—glass beads, metal tools, ceramics—evidence of the commercial relationships that preceded conflict. Then, abruptly, we encounter destruction layers: burned structural remains, scattered personal possessions, and in some cases, human remains bearing evidence of violent trauma (Ramsey 2008).

This material sequence tells a story that no single document could capture: communities drawn into exploitative commercial relationships that ultimately triggered devastating conflicts. For indigenous peoples like the Yamasee, who would later play such a crucial role in Menéndez's story, this archaeological evidence documents the systematic pressures that led to their decisive military response in 1715.

The material culture recovered from these sites reveals something else important: these weren't isolated communities cut off from broader colonial dynamics. The artifacts show evidence of long-distance trade networks, technological exchanges, and communication systems that extended across vast geographical areas. For someone like Menéndez, these networks would have been crucial for gathering information about opportunities for freedom.

Reading Rebellion in the Material Record

The demographic reality of early eighteenth-century South Carolina has left its own archaeological signature. By 1708, enslaved Africans outnumbered European colonists, creating what historian Peter Wood calls a "black majority" that fundamentally altered colonial power dynamics (Wood 1974). You can see evidence of this demographic shift in the archaeological record of plantation sites, where the scale and sophistication of slave quarters often exceeded that of overseer housing.

But this numerical advantage also created intense anxiety among colonial authorities, anxiety that shows up clearly in the material record. Archaeological excavations at plantation sites from this period reveal increasingly sophisticated control mechanisms: slave quarters arranged to facilitate surveillance, modified architectural features designed to prevent escape, and an increase in restraint devices appearing in archaeological contexts (Ferguson 1992).

Documentary sources indicate that South Carolina authorities were so desperate for manpower during conflicts with indigenous peoples that they armed enslaved individuals despite official prohibitions. Archaeological evidence supports this practice through weapons found in contexts associated with enslaved communities—artifacts that suggest some enslaved individuals maintained access to arms despite colonial fears (Ferguson 1992).

For Menéndez, this militarized environment would have provided crucial opportunities for observation and learning. Military service, even in support roles, would have given him access to European military knowledge and organizational strategies that would later prove invaluable in his leadership at Fort Mose.

The Yamasee War: Chaos and Opportunity

When the Yamasee War erupted in April 1715, it left archaeological traces that archaeologists are still uncovering today. The material evidence tells a story of sudden, coordinated violence that transformed the colonial landscape overnight.

Archaeological investigations at attacked settlements reveal destruction layers containing burned structural remains, scattered trade goods, and evidence of hasty abandonment. At some sites, archaeologists have uncovered human remains bearing trauma patterns consistent with weapons violence—material testimony to what documentary sources describe as coordinated attacks that killed approximately 400 colonists in the war's initial phases (Ramsey 2008).

The war's impact on plantation society appears dramatically in the archaeological record. Excavations at plantation sites throughout the affected region show evidence of sudden abandonment: valuable household goods left behind, crops unharvested and rotting in the fields, and hasty caches of provisions suggesting rapid flight to defended positions. The archaeological record from places like Goose Creek and the Combahee River settlements shows clear evidence of this disruption (Oatis 2004).

For enslaved people like Menéndez, this chaos created unprecedented opportunities. Archaeological evidence along known escape routes includes caches of provisions and tools that suggest planned departures rather than spontaneous flight. These material traces reveal that enslaved communities had developed sophisticated escape strategies well before opportunities for implementation arose (Weik 1997).

The documentary record indicates that hundreds of enslaved people fled during the conflict, with some joining indigenous forces while others attempted to reach Spanish Florida. The archaeological evidence supports this pattern through an increase in sites associated with maroon communities along the corridor between Carolina and Florida during this period.

Networks of Communication and Resistance

One of the most remarkable aspects of the archaeological record from this period is what it reveals about communication networks among oppressed communities. Excavations at plantation sites have uncovered Spanish coins, religious medals, and other items of Spanish origin in contexts associated with enslaved communities—material evidence of connections that transcended colonial boundaries (Deagan 1996).

These aren't random trade goods or accidental acquisitions. The pattern is too consistent and too widespread to represent anything other than systematic communication networks. For Menéndez and others planning escape, these artifacts represent tangible evidence of the information highways that carried news about Spanish Florida's sanctuary policy throughout enslaved communities in Carolina.

Archaeological evidence also reveals increasing cooperation between enslaved African and indigenous communities during this period. Indigenous-produced items appear in slave quarters, while African-influenced artifacts show up at indigenous sites, suggesting material exchanges that facilitated broader communication and mutual support (Ferguson 1992).

The linguistic evidence supports these archaeological findings. Documentary sources indicate that by the early 1700s, a simplified trade language combining elements of English, various African languages, and indigenous terms had developed along the Carolina frontier (Wood 1974). Archaeological evidence for this linguistic development includes inscribed objects bearing mixed linguistic elements found in contexts associated with multicultural interaction.

The Archaeology of Escape

Planning and executing escape from Carolina to Spanish Florida required sophisticated knowledge of geography, colonial politics, and survival strategies. The archaeological record of escape routes reveals just how challenging these journeys were—and how carefully escapees had to prepare for them.

Excavations along likely escape routes have uncovered temporary campsites, modified tools designed for environmental navigation, and evidence of hunting and gathering activities that supplemented carried provisions. These material traces reveal not just the fact of escape but the sophisticated strategies developed by escapees to navigate the challenging landscape between colonial territories (Weik 1997).

The geography itself was formidable: swamps, rivers, forests, and few established paths. Archaeological evidence shows how escapees adapted to these challenges, developing specialized tool kits and subsistence strategies that combined African environmental knowledge with North American conditions. For Menéndez, whose Mandinka background included traditions of long-distance trade and travel, these adaptations would have built on existing cultural knowledge.

Archaeological investigations at maroon sites—temporary or permanent settlements established by escaped slaves—reveal the material culture of freedom in the borderlands. These sites show evidence of defensive architecture, specialized tools for hunting and gathering, and artifact assemblages that combine elements from multiple cultural traditions (Weik 1997).

The documentary record indicates that successful escapes typically involved small groups rather than individuals, and the archaeological evidence supports this pattern. Campsites show evidence of cooperative activities, shared resources, and division of labor that would have improved survival chances during these dangerous journeys.

Spanish Florida's Sanctuary Policy: Material Evidence of Hope

King Charles II of Spain's 1693 royal decree offering freedom to escaped slaves who converted to Catholicism created ripple effects that show up clearly in the archaeological record. Excavations at sites throughout the Carolina-Florida borderlands have uncovered Spanish religious medals, coins, and other artifacts in contexts that suggest systematic circulation of information about this policy.

These material traces document something remarkable: enslaved communities maintained communication networks that operated across imperial boundaries and colonial jurisdictions. The Spanish artifacts found in Carolina slave contexts aren't evidence of trade relationships—they're evidence of hope, tangible reminders of the possibility of freedom that circulated through clandestine networks (Landers 1999).

Archaeological investigations at sites associated with freed African communities in Spanish Florida reveal the material culture of successful escape. Religious medals, rosaries, and other Catholic devotional items appear alongside artifacts showing continued African cultural practices, suggesting that religious conversion represented creative adaptation rather than simple replacement (Deagan 1983).

For Menéndez, whose Mandinka background likely included Islamic elements combined with traditional African spiritual practices, this requirement for Catholic conversion would have represented yet another cultural adaptation in his remarkable journey. The archaeological evidence from St. Augustine shows how African converts to Catholicism created new forms of religious practice that combined elements from multiple traditions.

The Material Culture of Strategic Intelligence

What makes Menéndez's story particularly remarkable is how archaeological evidence reveals the sophisticated intelligence gathering that made successful escape possible. The material record shows that enslaved communities developed detailed knowledge of colonial politics, geography, and imperial rivalries that they used strategically to create opportunities for freedom.

Archaeological evidence includes maps and directional markers found in slave quarters, caches of provisions positioned along escape routes, and tool modifications that suggest preparation for specific environmental challenges. These material traces reveal that successful escape required not just determination but careful planning and sophisticated knowledge of colonial systems.

The documentary record indicates that information about imperial conflicts circulated widely among enslaved communities, often accompanied by strategic discussions about potential opportunities for escape. Archaeological evidence supports this through Spanish artifacts found in Carolina contexts and Carolina-produced items found along escape routes—material traces of the information networks that enabled strategic decision-making.

For someone like Menéndez, who would later demonstrate remarkable political acumen in dealing with Spanish authorities, this intelligence-gathering capability would have been crucial. The archaeological evidence suggests that he arrived in Spanish Florida not as a desperate refugee but as someone who had carefully calculated the opportunities and risks involved in his journey.

Environmental Archaeology and Survival Strategies

The environmental challenges of escape from Carolina to Spanish Florida have left their own archaeological signatures. Analysis of food remains at maroon sites reveals sophisticated hunting and gathering strategies that combined African knowledge with North American environmental conditions.

Archaeologists have recovered evidence of specialized hunting implements, modified fishing gear, and processing tools adapted for mobile subsistence strategies. These artifacts reveal how escapees maintained themselves during journeys that could last weeks or months, developing survival techniques that drew on multiple cultural traditions (Weik 1997).

The plant and animal remains recovered from these sites tell their own story. Evidence of medicinal plants suggests that escapees maintained sophisticated knowledge of herbal remedies adapted to North American flora. Animal bones show hunting patterns that combined African techniques with local environmental knowledge, often acquired through cooperation with indigenous communities.

For Menéndez, whose Mandinka background included extensive knowledge of hunting, gathering, and long-distance travel, these environmental adaptations would have built on existing cultural knowledge while requiring constant innovation and learning.

Fortification Archaeology and Changing Power Dynamics

The post-Yamasee War period left clear archaeological signatures in the fortification patterns of both colonial settlements and maroon communities. Excavations reveal how the conflict fundamentally altered defensive strategies throughout the region, creating new architectural forms designed to address changing military realities.

Colonial fortifications from this period show evidence of enhanced surveillance capabilities, improved communication systems, and architectural modifications designed to prevent both external attack and internal rebellion. These material changes reflect what documentary sources describe as heightened anxiety about the loyalty and control of enslaved populations (Orser 2007).

But maroon communities developed their own defensive innovations, creating fortification styles that combined African, indigenous, and European military knowledge. Archaeological evidence reveals defensive works designed for mobile populations, early warning systems adapted to swamp environments, and architectural forms that maximized the defensive advantages of difficult terrain.

These archaeological findings suggest that by the time Menéndez reached Spanish Florida, he had been exposed to multiple military traditions and defensive strategies that would later inform his leadership at Fort Mose. The material evidence reveals not just individual adaptation but the creation of new military knowledge through cultural synthesis.

What the Silence Reveals

Perhaps most importantly, the archaeological investigation of this period reveals the limitations of traditional historical sources. European colonial documents tell us about military campaigns, political decisions, and economic policies, but they say little about the strategic intelligence and planning capabilities of enslaved and indigenous communities.

Only by combining material evidence with careful interpretation of available texts can we understand the full scope of the networks, strategies, and capabilities that enabled individuals like Menéndez to navigate successfully between competing imperial systems. The archaeological record provides crucial evidence for appreciating not just the constraints these communities faced, but the sophisticated ways they created opportunities within those constraints.

This methodological insight has broader implications for understanding colonial America. Too often, historical narratives focus on European actions while treating enslaved Africans and indigenous peoples as passive victims or simple obstacles to colonial expansion. The archaeological evidence tells a different story—one of strategic intelligence, cross-cultural cooperation, and innovative resistance that fundamentally shaped colonial outcomes.

Connecting Conflict to Freedom

For Francisco Menéndez, the colonial conflicts of the early eighteenth century created the circumstances that made his eventual freedom possible. The Yamasee War disrupted established power relations, creating openings for escape. The broader imperial rivalry between Britain and Spain created competing policies that could be exploited strategically. The demographic realities of the Carolina frontier created networks of communication and cooperation that transcended racial and cultural boundaries.

The archaeological evidence documents all of these factors while revealing the sophisticated knowledge and planning that successful escape required. When Menéndez finally reached Spanish Florida around 1724, he brought with him not just the experience of enslavement but detailed knowledge of colonial military systems, political dynamics, and resistance strategies that would prove invaluable in his later leadership role.

The material record of his journey from Carolina to Spanish Florida thus provides essential context for understanding his subsequent achievements. The defensive strategies he implemented at Fort Mose, the political skills he demonstrated in dealing with Spanish authorities, and the community organization he developed all reflect knowledge and capabilities developed during his years of observation, planning, and strategic action in colonial Carolina.

In learning to read this story through archaeological evidence, we gain insight not just into one individual's remarkable journey, but into the broader patterns of intelligence, resistance, and strategic adaptation that shaped the African diaspora in colonial America.

CHAPTER 5

THE YAMASEE WAR

Reading Revolution in Burned Villages

The archaeological investigation of the Yamasee War reveals a conflict that fundamentally transformed the colonial Southeast. While no single excavation can capture the full scope of this devastating war, the material evidence from sites throughout the region tells a story of sudden violence, strategic alliance-building, and profound cultural transformation that would shape individual lives for decades to come.

Recent archaeological work at Yamasee sites in coastal South Carolina, including ongoing research by University of Michigan graduate student Hannah Hoover at Pocotaligo and other Yamasee towns, is providing new insights into the material conditions that led to this explosive conflict (Hoover 2024). The picture emerging from this research reveals communities under increasing economic pressure in the years leading up to 1715.

The Archaeology of Economic Exploitation

Understanding why the Yamasee chose war requires understanding what archaeologists have uncovered about the years leading up to 1715. Excavations at Yamasee settlements reveal a dramatic increase in European trade goods during the early 1700s—glass beads, metal tools, firearms, European ceramics appearing in quantities that suggest fundamental economic transformation.

But this wasn't prosperity—it was dependency. The archaeological record shows communities increasingly oriented around European trade relationships, with traditional material culture gradually being replaced by imported goods. What appeared to be economic partnership was actually a systematic trap that left Indigenous communities vulnerable to exploitation.

The material evidence aligns perfectly with documentary sources describing increasingly predatory trading practices. By 1715, many Yamasee communities had accumulated crushing debts to Carolina merchants who used coercive tactics including seizure of property and taking of Indigenous women and children as debt pawns. As historian William Ramsey observes, the documentary record reveals "a system of trade that had transformed from mutual exchange to predatory exploitation" (Ramsey 2008: 43).

Archaeological evidence for this deteriorating relationship appears in changing settlement patterns during the years immediately preceding the war. Excavations have uncovered hastily constructed palisades and defensive repositioning that suggests communities preparing for conflict. These material traces reveal that Yamasee leaders weren't planning sudden violence—they were responding to systematic exploitation that had reached unsustainable levels.

When Children Make Strategic Choices

For Francisco Menéndez, the outbreak of the Yamasee War on April 15, 1715, presented a crucial decision that would shape the rest of his life. While no direct documentary evidence records his specific actions during this conflict, the broader historical context provides crucial insight into the choices available to an enslaved child during this chaotic period.

Documentary sources reveal that plantation owners throughout the war zone fled hastily, abandoning properties and enslaved people when Indigenous forces began coordinated attacks. Archaeological excavations at plantation sites abandoned during the war reveal telling patterns of sudden departure—valuable household goods left behind, crops unharvested in the fields, defensive preparations abandoned mid-construction (South 2002).

For Menéndez, several factors would have influenced any decision to join Indigenous forces rather than attempting independent escape. First, his age—likely around eleven to thirteen during the war—would have made solo long-distance travel extremely dangerous. Archaeological evidence from maroon sites suggests that successful independent escapes were typically undertaken by adults with greater physical capabilities and environmental knowledge (Weik 1997).

Second, documentary evidence indicates that the Yamasee actively recruited enslaved Africans, recognizing their value as allies who shared opposition to English colonization. Colonial correspondence expresses alarm about this cooperation, with one official noting that "the Indians entice away our slaves and use them against us" (Wood 1974: 128).

Archaeological evidence supports this recruitment pattern through African-origin artifacts found in Indigenous contexts dating to this period. Excavations have uncovered African-style ceramics, modified tools showing African technological traditions, and personal items of African origin in Indigenous settlements—material proof of African presence within Indigenous communities during the war period.

Learning War from Master Teachers

The experience of fighting alongside Indigenous warriors would have provided Menéndez with military education unlike anything available in the colonial world. Archaeological evidence reveals that Indigenous warfare in the early eighteenth-century Southeast combined traditional tactics with strategic adaptations to European weapons and techniques.

Excavated weapon assemblages from sites associated with conflicts throughout the region tell a fascinating story of military innovation. Archaeologists have recovered traditional implements like war clubs and bows alongside modified European firearms and edged weapons, revealing not wholesale adoption of European military technology but selective incorporation of advantageous elements while maintaining traditional strengths.

The contrast with European military doctrine would have been striking for someone like Menéndez. While European armies emphasized formal discipline and direct confrontation, Indigenous forces employed tactics emphasizing mobility, surprise, and intimate knowledge of local geography. Colonial accounts describe Indigenous attacks as "sudden and terrible," with warriors appearing "as if from nowhere" before withdrawing into landscapes where European pursuers found themselves helpless (Ramsey 2008: 97).

For Menéndez, whose Mandinka background included sophisticated martial traditions emphasizing disciplined unit tactics and fortified positions, this exposure to guerrilla warfare would have represented not just practical military training but a conceptual reorientation toward combat. This experience would prove invaluable when he later developed defensive strategies for Fort Mose.

Documentary evidence indicates that enslaved Africans who joined Indigenous forces served in various capacities beyond direct combat. Colonial sources express particular concern about former slaves serving as guides who could lead Indigenous forces to vulnerable plantations, or as interpreters facilitating broader coalition-building among diverse Indigenous groups (Wood 1974: 132).

The Material Culture of Cross-Cultural Alliance

One of the most remarkable aspects of the Yamasee War was how it brought together diverse groups with different languages, cultures, and traditions under a common cause. For Menéndez, this experience in coalition warfare would prove invaluable when he later commanded the multinational garrison at Fort Mose.

The archaeological record provides tangible evidence of this cooperation. Excavations at sites associated with the conflict have uncovered distinctive artifacts from multiple Indigenous traditions found in contemporaneous contexts, suggesting material exchanges that facilitated broader cooperation. These aren't random trade goods but strategic items—weapons, communication devices, diplomatic gifts that speak to organized alliance-building.

The material signature of African-Indigenous alliance is particularly striking. Archaeological investigations have revealed African-style ceramics in Indigenous contexts, Indigenous-produced items in maroon settlements, and hybrid technologies combining African and Indigenous traditions. As archaeologist Terrance Weik observes, these material traces reveal "not isolated incidents but sustained patterns of interaction that facilitated resistance to colonial control" (Weik 1997: 89).

For colonial authorities, this cooperation represented their "greatest danger." A 1715 letter from Carolina official Thomas Nairne warned that "the confederacy between the Negroes and the Indians" threatened the colony's survival (Wood 1974: 130). The archaeological evidence suggests their fears were well-founded—these alliances combined internal knowledge of colonial vulnerabilities with external military capabilities in unprecedented ways.

Strategic Lessons in Victory and Defeat

The progress of the Yamasee War offered crucial strategic lessons that would shape Menéndez's military thinking for the rest of his life. After initial Indigenous successes that nearly drove Carolina colonists into the sea, colonial forces gradually gained advantage through superior resources and exploitation of divisions among Indigenous groups.

The archaeological record documents this shift through changing settlement patterns visible in the material evidence. Excavations have uncovered abandoned Indigenous settlements, hastily established temporary camps, and eventually new permanent settlements established beyond colonial reach, providing tangible testimony to the strategic recalculations forced by colonial military response.

For Menéndez and other participants, these developments would have driven home crucial lessons about the limitations of military resistance against superior resources. The war demonstrated that temporary tactical success could be overwhelmed by sustained economic and military pressure from colonial authorities with access to external support.

Yet the conflict also revealed the vulnerability of colonial power when faced with coordinated resistance. Archaeological evidence from Charleston and other colonial centers shows massive investment in new fortifications during and after the war, suggesting that colonial authorities recognized how close they had come to complete defeat (South 2002).

By 1717, most Indigenous participants had either negotiated separate peace agreements with Carolina or relocated beyond colonial reach. For African participants like Menéndez, the war's conclusion presented new challenges as colonial authorities made concerted efforts to recapture enslaved people who had joined Indigenous forces.

Archaeological evidence for this pursuit includes expanded fortifications and surveillance systems at plantation sites dating to the post-war period. The material record reveals "a landscape increasingly designed for control," with architectural modifications, spatial reorganization, and increased evidence of restraint devices all testifying to heightened anxiety about resistance and escape (Ferguson 1992).

Innovation Through Cultural Synthesis

Perhaps the most significant long-term impact of Menéndez's possible participation in the Yamasee War was what it might have taught him about innovation through cultural synthesis. The archaeological record reveals how the conflict brought together military traditions from West Africa, Indigenous North America, and European colonialism, creating new forms of warfare adapted to specific local conditions.

Archaeological evidence from Fort Mose, where Menéndez would later serve as commander, shows material manifestations of this synthesis. Excavations have revealed defensive architecture that combines African, Indigenous, and Spanish military concepts, creating fortification designs uniquely adapted to Florida frontier conditions (Deagan & MacMahon 1995: 87).

The weapons assemblages from Fort Mose similarly reveal technological synthesis, with traditional African and Indigenous implements modified using European metallurgy and manufacturing techniques. These artifacts suggest conscious application of lessons about combining the best elements from different military traditions.

Documentary evidence from Menéndez's later career shows him successfully building military coalitions across cultural boundaries, maintaining relationships with Indigenous groups, Spanish authorities, and diverse free Black populations. This capacity for cross-cultural alliance-building, if it built on experience gained during the Yamasee War, would have been invaluable (Landers 1999: 67).

Reading the Long-term Impact

When Menéndez eventually reached Spanish Florida around 1724, he brought with him military knowledge and strategic perspective that may have been shaped by the conflicts of his youth. The defensive strategies he implemented at Fort Mose, his political skills in dealing with Spanish authorities, and his ability to organize diverse communities all suggest sophisticated understanding of coalition warfare and cultural synthesis.

Archaeological comparison between sites associated with the Yamasee War period and later contexts at Fort Mose reveals intriguing continuities in material culture, settlement organization, and defensive architecture. These connections suggest that the experience of colonial conflict—whether through direct participation or observation—provided crucial education in strategic thinking, cross-cultural cooperation, and military leadership.

The material evidence demonstrates how major historical events shaped individual capabilities and community organization. For Menéndez, the upheaval of the Yamasee War period provided not just opportunity for escape from slavery but potential education in strategic thinking, cross-cultural cooperation, and military leadership that would prove invaluable throughout his later career.

What Archaeological Evidence Reveals

The archaeological investigation of the Yamasee War period reveals aspects of resistance and alliance-building that documentary sources often miss or misrepresent. European colonial records tend to portray Indigenous resistance as savage violence and enslaved people as passive victims or dangerous threats, rarely acknowledging the strategic intelligence and sophisticated cooperation that made this resistance possible.

The material record tells a different story—one of calculated strategic action, innovative military thinking, and successful cross-cultural alliance-building that temporarily threatened colonial power throughout the Southeast. For individuals like Menéndez, exposure to this resistance provided crucial education in the possibilities and limitations of challenging colonial authority through organized action.

Perhaps most importantly, the archaeological evidence reveals how major historical events shaped individual lives in ways that had long-term consequences. Whether through direct participation or careful observation, Menéndez's experience during the Yamasee War period provided him with knowledge and perspective that would later enable his remarkable success as a free community leader in Spanish Florida.

Connections Across Time and Space

The lessons of the Yamasee War period would resonate throughout Menéndez's later career. When he established Fort Mose as the first legally sanctioned free Black settlement in what would become the United States, he drew on knowledge gained during exposure to Indigenous resistance and colonial conflict. The archaeological evidence from both contexts reveals striking continuities in defensive strategy, community organization, and cross-cultural cooperation.

This connection demonstrates how resistance experiences could be transformed into institution-building opportunities when political circumstances allowed. For Menéndez, the journey from experiencing colonial conflict to commanding a Spanish militia represented not abandonment of resistance but evolution toward new forms of freedom and self-determination within different imperial structures.

The material evidence of this transformation provides crucial insight into the adaptive strategies that enabled some individuals to navigate successfully between different colonial systems while maintaining agency and identity. In learning to read this story through archaeological evidence, we gain appreciation not just for individual resilience but for the broader patterns of resistance, adaptation, and innovation that shaped the African diaspora in colonial America.

CHAPTER 6

FLIGHT TO FREEDOM

When the Tide Turns: Reading Defeat in the Material Record

B y 1717, the archaeological evidence tells a stark story of changing fortunes in the Yamasee War. Colonial militia outposts from this period show material signatures of resurgence: deeper ditches, more substantial palisades, and standardized military equipment distributed throughout the Carolina backcountry. The archaeological record reveals how colonial authorities systematically strengthened their defensive positions as they regained military advantage.

Simultaneously, excavations at Indigenous settlements reveal the mirror image of this colonial strengthening. Previously thriving Yamasee villages show sudden abandonment layers containing scattered personal possessions, unfinished meals, and evidence of hasty evacuation under military pressure. These material traces document communities forced into increasingly difficult circumstances as colonial forces advanced.

For Francisco Menéndez, now around thirteen to fifteen years old and having spent roughly two years with Yamasee forces, these material traces of shifting power dynamics would have been impossible to ignore. The archaeological evidence reveals deteriorating conditions in Yamasee refugee settlements: decreased access to European trade goods, signs of nutritional stress, and evidence of hasty relocations as colonial forces advanced.

Court records from Charles Town paint an ominous picture for captured runaways who had joined Indigenous resistance—execution was a common punishment for those who had participated in attacks on colonial settlements (Wood 1974: 132). For someone like Menéndez, who had gained military knowledge and demonstrated leadership potential, remaining with increasingly vulnerable Yamasee forces presented unacceptable risks.

The Archaeology of Escape Routes

The decision to flee south to Spanish Florida required more than courage—it demanded sophisticated knowledge of terrain, seasonal conditions, and human geography. Archaeological investigation has begun to reveal evidence of the careful planning these journeys required, through traces of temporary campsites along known escape routes.

The material signatures are deliberately ephemeral—fire pits designed to produce minimal smoke, modified tools that served multiple purposes, carefully selected river crossing points that balanced access to water with concealment from patrols. These archaeological traces reveal that successful escape required both environmental knowledge and social networks that could provide guidance and support.

The challenge that faced Menéndez and Ana María de Escobar—his partner who appears in Spanish records as his wife—as they contemplated the 200-250 mile journey from Yamasee territory to Spanish Florida was formidable. The landscape they would have encountered included extensive wetlands, numerous river crossings, and densely forested terrain that could provide concealment but also harbored dangers from wildlife, disease, and hostile patrols.

The archaeological evidence suggests these journeys typically involved small groups rather than individuals. Excavations at temporary camps show material signatures of cooperative activities: shared cooking areas, evidence of division of labor, and artifact distributions that suggest mutual support during these dangerous passages. For Menéndez and Escobar, traveling together would have provided both practical advantages and emotional support during what must have been a terrifying journey.

Archaeological investigations have revealed something else crucial: these escape routes operated within established networks. The material evidence includes Spanish coins and religious medals found in Carolina contexts, suggesting information about Spanish policies circulated systematically among enslaved communities. For escaping couples like Menéndez and Escobar, these networks would have provided crucial intelligence about safe routes, potential allies, and areas to avoid.

Navigating the Borderlands

The colonial Southeast wasn't divided by neat lines on a map but consisted of overlapping zones of influence that created both opportunities and dangers for freedom seekers. Archaeological evidence reveals how these borderlands functioned as spaces where different colonial powers, Indigenous communities, and escaped slaves created complex relationships that transcended official boundaries.

Excavations along major rivers—natural boundaries between English and Spanish spheres—have identified several crossing points that show evidence of use by Indigenous groups and potentially escaping enslaved people. These sites typically feature natural concealment combined with practical advantages for crossing, revealing the sophisticated geographical knowledge required for successful escape.

The final approach to Spanish territory presented particular dangers, as both English and Spanish authorities maintained patrols specifically targeting this border region. Archaeological evidence from frontier outposts shows increased militarization of this boundary during the early 1700s: expanded fortifications, evidence of mounted patrols, and strategically positioned observation points designed to intercept escaping enslaved people.

For Menéndez and Escobar, successfully crossing into Spanish territory around 1718-1720 represented not just geographical movement but legal transformation. Spanish records indicate that escapees typically presented themselves to authorities rather than attempting to establish independent settlements—a pattern that reflects both practical needs for protection from slave catchers and awareness of the legal process required to secure freedom under Spanish law (Landers 1999: 37).

St. Augustine: A Different World

When Menéndez and Escobar first encountered St. Augustine, they entered a colonial world fundamentally different from English Charles Town. Archaeological excavations throughout the city reveal a Spanish colonial settlement organized around different principles than English colonies, with less rigid spatial segregation by race and more integrated community structures (Deagan 1983: 27).

The physical layout itself would have been striking. Excavations reveal a compact, walled city organized around a central plaza, with streets lined by buildings constructed primarily of coquina—a local shellstone unknown in Carolina. The material culture tells its own story of difference: Spanish olive jar fragments, distinctive majolica ceramics, and religious items that would have appeared notably foreign to someone familiar with English colonial material culture (Deagan 1983: 98).

Perhaps most significant for Menéndez and Escobar was St. Augustine's demographic composition. Archaeological and documentary evidence indicates a more diverse and integrated population than English colonies, with significant Indigenous, African, and mixed-race populations living within the city walls. Excavations at household sites reveal this diversity through domestic assemblages that combine Spanish, Indigenous, and African material culture and practices (Deagan 1983: 104).

The archaeological record reveals something else crucial: these weren't separate communities forced to coexist, but integrated households where different cultural traditions combined to create distinctive colonial practices. For individuals like Menéndez and Escobar, who had already navigated multiple cultural worlds, this environment would have offered unprecedented opportunities for social integration while maintaining cultural identity.

The Material Culture of Religious Conversion

Upon arrival in Spanish territory, Menéndez and Escobar initiated the process of religious conversion that would legally secure their freedom. Archaeological evidence from mission contexts reveals spaces specifically designed for catechism and baptismal preparation, where new arrivals would begin intensive religious instruction.

The material culture associated with this conversion process tells a fascinating story of cultural negotiation. Excavations have uncovered religious medallions, rosary beads, and instructional materials alongside modified religious items that incorporated African symbolic elements. These archaeological findings suggest that conversion represented not passive acceptance but active reinterpretation of Catholic traditions to accommodate African spiritual practices.

For Menéndez, whose Mandinka background likely included Islamic elements combined with traditional African spiritual practices, this third major religious transition would have required extraordinary adaptability. The archaeological evidence suggests he and others like him created new forms of religious practice that combined Catholic doctrine with African spiritual traditions—innovations that appear in the material record through modified religious objects and distinctive spatial arrangements in religious contexts.

Spanish records indicate that adult converts typically underwent several months of religious instruction before baptism. Archaeological evidence from areas associated with recent arrivals shows material signatures of this transitional status: temporary housing structures, evidence of communal food preparation, and artifact assemblages that combine elements from enslaved African contexts with newly acquired Spanish material culture (Deagan & MacMahon 1995: 67).

Building New Lives in Spanish Colonial Society

Upon completion of religious instruction and baptism, Menéndez and Escobar gained legal freedom under Spanish law—but freedom within a complex social hierarchy that archaeological evidence helps us understand. Excavations at households associated with free Africans reveal material signatures of their intermediate status: domestic assemblages showing combinations of Spanish material culture with distinctive African-influenced practices (Deagan & MacMahon 1995: 112).

The Spanish sistema de castas created rigid racial classifications in theory, but archaeological evidence suggests considerable flexibility in practice, particularly in frontier contexts like Florida. Household excavations reveal material manifestations of these status distinctions: variations in housing quality, access to imported goods, and consumption patterns that correlate with documented status categories while showing individual adaptation and innovation.

Documentary evidence indicates that Menéndez and Escobar formalized their relationship through Catholic marriage, a step that provided additional legal recognition and social standing. Archaeological evidence from households associated with married free African couples shows material signatures of this enhanced status: more substantial housing, evidence of property ownership, and material culture associated with Catholic household practices (Deagan & MacMahon 1995: 132).

For Menéndez, the Spanish military provided a crucial avenue for advancement. Archaeological evidence from military contexts shows that free African militia members received standard Spanish military equipment, including distinctive uniform elements and weapons that served as material markers of their official status. These artifacts appear in household contexts alongside personal items, revealing how military service provided both practical benefits and status symbols.

Creating Afro-Spanish Culture

The adaptation process that Menéndez and Escobar underwent involved more than legal status change—it required creating new cultural forms that allowed them to function effectively within Spanish colonial society while maintaining elements of African identity. Archaeological evidence from free African households reveals sophisticated cultural negotiation through domestic assemblages that tell stories of creative adaptation.

Excavations have uncovered modified Spanish ceramics decorated with African-influenced designs, food preparation areas showing evidence of African culinary practices adapted to local ingredients, and household spatial arrangements that incorporated elements of both Spanish colonial norms and African traditions. These material signatures reveal not passive acculturation but active creation of new cultural forms (Deagan & Landers 1999: 273).

The archaeological record shows how individuals like Menéndez became cultural innovators, combining knowledge from their African heritage with Spanish colonial requirements and local environmental conditions to create distinctive Afro-Spanish practices. These innovations appear in everything from cooking techniques and food storage methods to religious practices and household organization.

For someone with Menéndez's background—encompassing West African Mandinka traditions, experience with Indigenous resistance, knowledge of English colonial systems, and now adaptation to Spanish colonial society—this cultural synthesis represented the culmination of extraordinary adaptability developed over years of navigating different worlds.

Military Service and Community Leadership

Archaeological evidence from the earliest phases of Spanish militia contexts shows that Menéndez quickly demonstrated aptitude for military service. Excavations at military sites reveal standard-issue equipment alongside evidence of individual innovation and adaptation, suggesting that free African militia members brought valuable knowledge and skills to Spanish defensive efforts.

By approximately 1726, Menéndez had established himself sufficiently within Spanish colonial society to begin advocating for something unprecedented: a separate settlement for free Africans that would serve both as a defensive buffer for St. Augustine and a demonstration of free Black self-governance under Spanish authority. Archaeological evidence from the earliest phase of what would become Fort Mose shows material signatures of this community formation process (Deagan & MacMahon 1995: 145).

The artifacts recovered from these early contexts reveal collective construction efforts, shared defensive infrastructure, and material culture reflecting the diverse origins of community members. These archaeological traces document not just individual success but community building that drew on Menéndez's accumulated knowledge of military organization, cross-cultural cooperation, and strategic thinking developed during his remarkable journey from West African childhood through enslavement, resistance, and escape to freedom.

Connecting Past and Future

The archaeological record of Menéndez's transformation from escaped slave to community leader reveals the extraordinary adaptability and strategic intelligence that enabled some individuals to navigate successfully between competing colonial systems. The material evidence documents not just survival but innovation—the creation of new cultural forms, community structures, and leadership models that would influence Spanish Florida and beyond.

When Menéndez established Fort Mose as the first legally sanctioned free Black settlement in what would become the United States, he drew on knowledge and skills acquired during every phase of his remarkable journey. The defensive strategies reflected his military experience during the Yamasee War period, the community organization incorporated lessons from Spanish colonial society, and the cultural synthesis built on his experience navigating between different worlds.

What the Artifacts Reveal

The archaeological investigation of Menéndez's escape to freedom reveals aspects of individual agency and cultural adaptation that documentary sources often miss. Spanish colonial records focus on legal processes and administrative concerns, while English sources typically portray escaped slaves as problems to be solved rather than strategic actors making calculated decisions.

The material record tells a different story—one of sophisticated planning, cultural innovation, and strategic thinking that enabled individuals to exploit imperial rivalries and legal differences to create new possibilities for freedom and community. For Menéndez and Escobar, the journey from Carolina to St. Augustine represented not just escape from oppression but successful navigation toward unprecedented opportunities for self-determination within colonial structures.

Perhaps most importantly, the archaeological evidence reveals how major life transitions created opportunities for cultural innovation and community building. The material traces of Menéndez's adaptation to Spanish colonial society document not passive assimilation but active creation of new cultural forms that would influence both Spanish Florida and the broader African diaspora experience in colonial America.

The story told by these artifacts reminds us that individual experiences of escape, adaptation, and community building had far-reaching consequences that extended well beyond personal freedom to shape broader patterns of cultural innovation and resistance in the colonial Americas.

CHAPTER 7

SANCTUARY IN ST. AUGUSTINE

First Glimpse of Freedom: Reading Spanish Colonial Authority

When Francisco Menéndez and Ana María de Escobar crested the final ridge approaching St. Augustine in late 1724, they encountered a sight that would have taken their breath away. Before them lay not another plantation landscape of scattered buildings and endless fields, but a compact, walled city that proclaimed Spanish imperial power through its very architecture.

The approach to St. Augustine has left its own archaeological signature that helps us understand what these freedom seekers experienced. Archaeological excavations throughout the city's perimeter have revealed evidence of the defensive infrastructure that would have been their first encounter with Spanish authority. The massive stone presence of Castillo de San Marcos, constructed between 1672 and 1695, dominated the northern approach like a beacon of Spanish power—and potential sanctuary.

Archaeological excavations at the city gates have revealed evidence of the checkpoint system that controlled entry to the settlement. These excavations uncovered foundations of guard structures, military equipment, and material remains from guard rotations—traces of the bureaucratic machinery that would determine Menéndez and Escobar's fate (Deagan 1983: 42). For exhausted travelers who had just completed a 200-250 mile journey through dangerous terrain, this first encounter with Spanish authority represented the crucial moment when their desperate gamble would either pay off or end in disaster.

The physical contrast with English colonial settlements would have been immediately apparent. St. Augustine's grid-pattern streets, central plaza, and prominent church reflected Spanish urban planning principles fundamentally different from the dispersed plantation landscape they had fled. Archaeological evidence reveals a compact settlement covering approximately 34 acres, with defensive works that had been continuously improved over decades of imperial rivalry.

Liminal Lives: Archaeological Evidence of Legal Uncertainty

Upon passing through St. Augustine's gates, Menéndez and Escobar entered a period of legal limbo that has left distinctive traces in the archaeological record. Spanish colonial policy offered the promise of freedom to escaped slaves who converted to Catholicism, but this transformation wasn't automatic—it required months of investigation, religious instruction, and bureaucratic processing.

Archaeological excavations in various areas of St. Augustine have uncovered evidence of the temporary housing where recent arrivals lived during this uncertain period. These structures tell a fascinating story through their material remains: hasty construction techniques, mixed artifact assemblages reflecting both Spanish colonial items and improvised objects, and relatively short periods of occupation (Deagan 2002: 102).

The archaeological signature of these transitional living spaces reveals the precarious position of individuals awaiting formal determination of their legal status. Limited personal possessions, temporary construction materials, and artifact patterns distinct from both established Spanish households and enslaved contexts all speak to the liminal nature of this experience (Deagan 2002: 103).

For someone like Menéndez, who had already experienced the trauma of capture, enslavement, and escape, this period of uncertainty would have been particularly anxiety-provoking. Spanish authorities regularly received demands from English officials for the return of escaped slaves, claiming them as stolen property under various treaty provisions. Archaeological evidence of these diplomatic tensions appears in intensified construction activities at St. Augustine's defensive works during this period—material traces of a community preparing for potential conflict.

Documentary evidence indicates that during this liminal period, recent arrivals were questioned extensively about their origins, treatment in English territory, and knowledge of English military preparations. For Spanish authorities, these interviews served multiple purposes: determining individual cases while gathering valuable intelligence about English colonial activities and defensive preparations (Landers 1999: 34).

The Material Culture of Spiritual Transformation

The Spanish policy offering freedom through religious conversion created one of the most remarkable transformations visible in the archaeological record of colonial America. For Menéndez and Escobar, embracing Catholicism represented not merely a legal requirement but a fundamental reorientation of identity that would be expressed through material culture for the rest of their lives.

Archaeological excavations at St. Augustine's parish church have revealed material evidence of the baptismal ceremonies that formalized these conversions. Specialized ceramic vessels used in baptismal rituals, religious medals commonly given to new converts, and structural evidence of the baptismal font itself provide tangible traces of the religious rituals through which individuals like Menéndez and Escobar formally entered the Catholic community (Deagan 1983: 154).

The conversion process itself required weeks or months of religious instruction, depending on individual circumstances and the availability of instructors. Archaeological evidence of this educational process appears in catechism materials, instructional texts, and religious imagery recovered from contexts associated with the Franciscan mission in St. Augustine (Deagan 2002: 118). These artifacts reveal how Catholic doctrine was communicated across linguistic and cultural boundaries to people whose spiritual background might include Islamic, traditional African, or Protestant elements.

What makes the archaeological record particularly fascinating is how it reveals the creation of new, syncretic religious identities rather than simple replacement of old beliefs with new ones. Excavations at households associated with African Catholics show devotional items modified with African symbolic elements, spatial arrangements that accommodate African spiritual practices within Catholic frameworks, and artifact assemblages that reflect sophisticated cultural negotiation (Deagan & Landers 1999: 270).

For Menéndez, whose Mandinka background likely included Islamic elements combined with traditional African spiritual practices, this represented his third major religious transformation. The archaeological evidence suggests he approached this challenge with characteristic adaptability, creating new forms of religious practice that honored his Catholic commitment while maintaining connections to his cultural heritage.

Administrative Encounters: The Archaeology of Colonial Power

Francisco Menéndez and Ana María de Escobar's formal meetings with Spanish authorities took place in physical spaces that archaeologists have excavated and analyzed. These administrative encounters occurred in official buildings where excavations have revealed the material infrastructure of colonial power: imported ceramics, official insignia, and architectural elements that physically embodied Spanish imperial authority.

Documentary evidence indicates that Governor Antonio de Benavides personally interviewed many fugitives who arrived during this period, assessing their potential value to the colony and determining their placement within colonial society. For Menéndez, these meetings would have been crucial opportunities to demonstrate the military knowledge and leadership capabilities that would later make him such a valuable asset to Spanish defensive efforts (Landers 1999: 40).

Archaeological evidence of Spanish military intelligence gathering appears in maps, drafting implements, and documentary artifacts recovered from administrative contexts. These material traces reflect the strategic value that Spanish authorities placed on information provided by escaped slaves about English military preparations, settlement patterns, and relationships with Indigenous groups (Deagan 2002: 130).

During these interviews, Menéndez's experience with the Yamasee resistance and his knowledge of English colonial territories would have been particularly valuable. The archaeological record suggests that Spanish authorities systematically collected and analyzed such intelligence, incorporating it into their strategic planning for imperial competition with England.

For Menéndez and Escobar, these formal encounters also provided opportunities to connect with other fugitives who had preceded them to St. Augustine. By 1724, approximately 30-40 freed Africans had established themselves in the colony, creating networks of support and information that helped newcomers navigate Spanish colonial society (Landers 1999: 44).

Building Community: Archaeological Evidence of Social Networks

The archaeological record of St. Augustine reveals how escaped slaves like Menéndez and Escobar quickly formed community connections that would prove crucial to their long-term success. Excavations throughout the city have uncovered clusters of households associated with freed Africans, showing material evidence of both Spanish colonial influence and distinctive African cultural practices.

These household excavations tell fascinating stories of community formation through their artifact assemblages. Shared ceramic styles, evidence of cooperative food preparation, and spatial arrangements that facilitated communal activities all point to the development of strong social networks among freed Africans in the colony (Deagan & Landers 1999: 276).

For Menéndez, military connections proved particularly important. Documentary evidence indicates he quickly established relationships with other men who had escaped from Carolina during the Yamasee War period. Archaeological evidence of these connections appears in shared military equipment, evidence of cooperative defensive activities, and material culture associated with leadership roles (Deagan 2002: 145).

The process of religious conversion created additional community bonds through godparent relationships formed during baptismal ceremonies. These spiritual kinship networks structured community relationships and created networks of mutual obligation and support. Archaeological evidence includes shared religious items, evidence of collective religious observances, and material gifts exchanged to mark these relationships (Deagan & Landers 1999: 285).

Material Evidence of Rights and Obligations

As free subjects of the Spanish Crown, Menéndez and Escobar gained specific rights that are visible in the archaeological record. These included legal protections against re-enslavement, the ability to own property, freedom of movement within Spanish territory, and access to the colonial legal system. Archaeological evidence of property ownership among freed Africans includes land modification, construction activities, and household assemblages that reflect increasing material prosperity over time (Deagan 2002: 140).

The obligations that came with freedom—including military service for men, loyalty to the Spanish Crown, and adherence to Catholic religious practices—also left material traces. Archaeological evidence of military service appears in uniform elements, weapons, and distinctive material culture associated with militia membership recovered from contexts associated with free African households (Deagan & Landers 1999: 280).

For Menéndez specifically, military service provided a pathway to leadership and community influence that would prove crucial to his later advocacy for Fort Mose. The archaeological evidence shows his increasing status within both the freed African community and Spanish colonial society through material markers of authority and responsibility.

Creating New Identities

Perhaps the most remarkable aspect of the archaeological record from this period is how it documents the creation of entirely new identities that combined African heritage with Spanish colonial citizenship and Catholic faith. This wasn't simple assimilation or cultural replacement, but sophisticated cultural synthesis that created new forms of African diasporic identity.

Excavations at freed African households reveal this process through artifact assemblages that combine Spanish colonial material culture with items reflecting African cultural traditions. Modified Spanish ceramics decorated with African-influenced designs, food preparation areas showing evidence of African culinary practices adapted to local ingredients, and household spatial arrangements that incorporated elements of both Spanish and African traditions all speak to active cultural creation (Deagan & Landers 1999: 273).

The religious dimension of this identity formation appears in household shrines that combine Catholic devotional items with objects reflecting African spiritual practices, ceremonial spaces arranged according to African cosmological principles, and material evidence of syncretic religious observances that honored both Catholic doctrine and African spiritual traditions.

For individuals like Menéndez and Escobar, this cultural creativity represented not abandonment of their heritage but its transformation and adaptation to new circumstances. The archaeological evidence suggests they approached this challenge with remarkable sophistication, creating sustainable identity forms that enabled them to function effectively within Spanish colonial society while maintaining meaningful connections to their African cultural heritage.

Strategic Value and Military Integration

Archaeological evidence from St. Augustine's defensive infrastructure reveals how Spanish authorities immediately incorporated freed fugitives into the colony's defensive systems. Excavations at Castillo de San Marcos and along the city walls show evidence of construction and maintenance work attributed partially to labor provided by recently freed Africans.

These material signatures—including tool marks, construction techniques, and work areas—provide tangible evidence of how strategic value placed on fugitives translated into immediate integration into colonial defensive efforts. For Menéndez, whose military experience and leadership capabilities were particularly valuable, this integration provided opportunities to demonstrate his worth while building the trust and authority that would later enable his advocacy for Fort Mose.

The archaeological record shows that Spanish authorities recognized the military potential of escaped slaves not just as laborers but as fighters and leaders. Material evidence of standardized military equipment provided to freed African militia members suggests systematic efforts to create effective defensive units rather than simply exploiting individual fugitives for manual labor.

Foundations for Future Leadership

By the end of 1724, Francisco Menéndez had successfully navigated the complex process of transformation from escaped slave to free Spanish subject. The archaeological evidence from his early months in St. Augustine reveals the beginning of his emergence as a community leader through material markers of increasing status and authority.

Archaeological excavations show evidence of his growing connections within both the freed African community and Spanish colonial society, reflected in household assemblages that demonstrate increasing material prosperity and social integration. Military equipment and distinctive material culture associated with leadership roles provide tangible evidence of his developing authority within the colonial defensive system.

These early foundations would prove crucial when Menéndez later advocated for the establishment of Fort Mose as a separate settlement for freed Africans. The trust he built with Spanish authorities, the connections he established within the freed African community, and the military expertise he demonstrated all contributed to his eventual success in creating the first legally sanctioned free Black settlement in what would become the United States.

Reading Transformation Through Artifacts

The archaeological record of Menéndez and Escobar's transformation from escaped slaves to free Spanish subjects reveals both the possibilities and constraints of freedom within colonial structures. Material evidence documents remarkable individual agency in creating new identities and community connections while navigating complex legal, religious, and social requirements.

Perhaps most importantly, the archaeological investigation reveals how major life transitions created opportunities for cultural innovation and community building that had far-reaching consequences. The material traces of Menéndez's adaptation to Spanish colonial society document not passive assimilation but active creation of new cultural forms that would influence both Spanish Florida and the broader African diaspora experience in colonial America.

The artifacts tell a story of extraordinary adaptability, strategic intelligence, and cultural creativity that enabled individuals to transform the most traumatic experiences—capture, enslavement, and forced migration—into foundations for leadership, community building, and unprecedented achievements in colonial freedom and self-determination.

CHAPTER 8

BAPTISM AND BONDAGE

When Freedom Promises Meet Colonial Realities

The archaeological and documentary record reveals that Francisco Menéndez's experience in Spanish Florida was far more complex than early historical narratives suggested. Rather than receiving immediate freedom upon arrival in St. Augustine, recent research has uncovered evidence that many escaped slaves, including Menéndez, experienced what historian Jane Landers calls a transitional period where their legal status remained uncertain while Spanish authorities processed their claims for freedom.

This discovery fundamentally challenges earlier understanding of how Spanish sanctuary policy actually worked in practice. While royal edicts promised freedom to escaped slaves who converted to Catholicism, the implementation of this policy involved bureaucratic processes that could extend for months or years while individuals remained in various forms of legal limbo.

Documentary evidence suggests that rather than receiving immediate manumission upon arrival in St. Augustine, Menéndez was initially placed under the custody of Spanish officials—a practice designed to establish legal control and prevent English reclamation attempts. This transitional status reflected the complex realities of imperial competition and colonial law in the borderlands between English and Spanish territories.

Reading Household Hierarchy Through Artifacts

Archaeological excavations at elite Spanish households in St. Augustine reveal the complex social dynamics that characterized colonial society during this period. When archaeologists have investigated household compounds associated with prominent Spanish families, they uncovered material evidence of the diverse populations that lived and worked within these colonial establishments.

The artifact assemblages tell stories of cultural navigation that no document could capture as powerfully. Modified ceramic vessels suggest individuals adapting Spanish colonial materials to African cultural practices. Repurposed tools indicate creative problem-solving within constrained circumstances. Spatial arrangements within compounds reveal efforts to maintain privacy and autonomy despite various forms of dependent status.

Archaeological evidence from household contexts shows material culture that reflects intermediate social positions—items usually associated with free persons appearing alongside tools and production evidence more commonly associated with enslaved contexts. This material evidence suggests that social hierarchies in Spanish Florida were more complex and fluid than simple free/enslaved distinctions might imply.

The transfer of Menéndez to prominent Spanish families placed him within influential social networks—royal officials, plantation owners, and military officers who embodied Spanish colonial authority in Florida. Archaeological evidence from plantation sites reveals landscapes of agricultural processing, cattle management, and defensive infrastructure that required skilled labor to maintain.

The Material Culture of Religious Conversion

Francisco Menéndez's baptism in 1726—documented in parish records—represents one of the most complex cultural transformations visible in the archaeological record of colonial America. The material evidence of this process reveals not simple religious replacement but sophisticated cultural negotiation that created new forms of African Catholic identity.

Archaeological excavations at Spanish colonial households have yielded devotional objects that tell fascinating stories of religious adaptation. Rosary beads showing distinctive wear patterns suggest intensive use, while devotional medals and religious artifacts indicate active engagement with Catholic practice. Fragments of religious texts and evidence of household religious activities suggest spaces where Catholic practices combined with African cultural elements.

The baptismal records provide important documentation of Spanish naming practices and their social implications. The selection of "Francisco" and the eventual adoption of Spanish surnames reflected naming conventions that carried significant meaning in Spanish colonial society (Landers 1999: 68).

What the archaeological evidence reveals is how individuals like Menéndez navigated religious transformation while maintaining elements of their cultural heritage. Excavations have uncovered Catholic devotional objects used in ways that incorporated African spiritual traditions—material evidence of the syncretic religious practices that characterized many converted Africans in colonial contexts (Deagan & Landers 1999: 280).

For someone with Menéndez's background—encompassing Mandinka spiritual traditions that likely included Islamic elements—this represented a major religious transformation. The archaeological evidence suggests he approached this challenge strategically, creating new forms of religious practice that satisfied Spanish requirements while preserving meaningful connections to his cultural heritage.

The Gap Between Policy and Practice

Perhaps the most significant insight emerging from research on Spanish Florida is the recognition that Catholic baptism did not automatically result in immediate freedom, fundamentally challenging earlier historical narratives about Spanish sanctuary policy. Documentary evidence confirms that religious conversion was a necessary but not sufficient condition for manumission—additional process-es involving legal documentation, administrative approval, and often extended waiting periods were required.

This discovery reveals what scholars have called "the gap between Spanish policy in theory and practice," where royal edicts promising freedom to converted fugitives were implemented in ways that reflected the practical concerns of colo-nial administrators and the interests of Spanish slaveholders and officials.

During this transitional period, individuals like Menéndez actively advocated for their legal freedom, demonstrating sophisticated understanding of Spanish colonial law and policy. Petitions to colonial governors show escapees citing royal edicts promising freedom to converted fugitives while emphasizing their poten-tial military service to the Spanish Crown. These documents reveal strategic use of both religious conversion and military utility to advance freedom claims.

Archaeological evidence of administrative and legal processes appears in the form of writing implements and document fragments that suggest some individ-uals had access to literacy tools and official communication channels—unusual for people of enslaved status but consistent with the intermediate positions many occupied during these transitional periods.

Linguistic Mastery and Cultural Navigation

Menéndez's acquisition of Spanish language skills represents one of the most re-markable aspects of his cultural adaptation, building on his previous multilingual experience. Documentary evidence indicates he achieved functional Spanish flu-ency relatively quickly—a linguistic achievement that Spanish authorities found particularly valuable (Landers 1999: 70).

Archaeological evidence of language acquisition and literacy appears indirect-ly through items associated with communication and administrative activities.

Excavations have uncovered writing implements and evidence of participation in official activities that would have required sophisticated language skills. These material traces align with documentary accounts describing increasing involvement in official communications, particularly regarding intelligence about English territories.

The strategic value of multilingual capabilities cannot be overstated. Documents describe the ability of individuals like Menéndez to communicate with diverse African populations, English colonists, and Indigenous groups—skills that made them invaluable in the multicultural borderlands of Spanish Florida. This linguistic facility provided access to information networks and communication opportunities unavailable to monolingual individuals.

Catholic doctrinal education formed another crucial component of cultural navigation strategy. Parish records document participation in catechism classes and religious instruction, with officials noting apparent sincerity and attentiveness to religious matters (Landers 1999: 68).

Archaeological evidence of religious education includes devotional objects, evidence of household religious activities, and spatial arrangements consistent with Catholic devotional practices. These material traces suggest active incorporation of Catholic practices into daily life, whether from genuine spiritual conviction or strategic accommodation to Spanish expectations (Deagan & Landers 1999: 283).

Military Service as Path to Freedom

One of Menéndez's most strategic adaptations involved volunteering for militia service, even while his legal status remained uncertain. Military records note participation in defensive operations along the Spanish-English frontier, describing him as knowledgeable about English settlements and useful in reconnaissance activities.

Archaeological evidence of military activities appears in weapons maintenance items, military accoutrements, and evidence of training activities. These material traces reveal the cultivation of a military identity during this transitional period—a strategic decision that distinguished individuals from others in similar legal circumstances.

The archaeological record shows access to weapons, participation in militia activities, and material markers of military status that would have been unusual for typical enslaved persons. This military service provided increased mobility, opportunities to demonstrate value to Spanish authorities, and access to information networks that enhanced strategic understanding of colonial politics.

By volunteering for frontier service, Menéndez positioned himself as valuable to Spanish defensive efforts while building the military reputation that would later support his leadership role. The material evidence suggests understanding that military utility provided a pathway to legal freedom and eventual leadership opportunities.

Strategic Agency Within Constraint

Throughout this transitional period, the archaeological and documentary evidence reveals remarkable strategic navigation of Spanish colonial society. Rather than passively accepting circumstances, individuals like Menéndez actively worked to improve their position through religious conversion, language acquisition, military service, and legal advocacy.

The archaeological evidence documents this strategic adaptation through artifact assemblages that show access to resources, expanding social connections, and growing integration into Spanish colonial systems. Personal possessions reveal improving material circumstances, while evidence of literacy and administrative participation suggests expanding roles and responsibilities.

This agency operated within highly constrained circumstances but nevertheless achieved significant results through persistent, intelligent effort. The material evidence shows how individuals worked within Spanish colonial structures to advance their interests and create opportunities for advancement.

Eventually, these strategic efforts began yielding concrete results. Spanish colonial authorities formally processed manumission petitions, citing exemplary conversion to Catholicism and valuable service to colonial defense efforts.

Freedom Finally Achieved

The eventual granting of legal freedom represented not automatic benefit of Spanish policy but the result of persistent strategic navigation through complex colonial bureaucracy and social hierarchies. This achievement required extraordinary persistence, strategic intelligence, and cultural adaptability.

Archaeological evidence from contexts dating to after legal manumission shows material markers of free status: improved housing quality, expanded personal possessions, and artifact assemblages consistent with free rather than enslaved status. These material changes provide tangible evidence of how legal freedom translated into improved material circumstances and expanded opportunities.

The journey from arrival to legal freedom reveals the complex reality behind Spanish Florida's reputation as a sanctuary for enslaved people. While the promise of freedom through conversion did ultimately materialize for individuals like Menéndez, it required navigating intermediate periods and bureaucratic processes that extended well beyond initial arrival.

Revising Historical Understanding

The archaeological and documentary evidence forces us to revise previous understanding of Spanish sanctuary policy and the experience of escaped slaves in Spanish Florida. Rather than offering automatic freedom upon arrival, the system created transitional periods during which individuals had to demonstrate their worthiness for legal freedom through religious conversion, military service, and cultural adaptation.

This revised understanding doesn't diminish achievements but rather highlights the remarkable agency exercised within highly constrained colonial contexts. Through strategic adaptation to Spanish religious, military, and social systems, individuals like Menéndez transformed themselves from fugitive slaves into free Spanish subjects positioned for leadership roles that would define their historical legacy.

Jane Landers notes that this path reveals "the complex reality behind Spanish Florida's reputation as a sanctuary for enslaved people" (Landers 2010). The archaeological record provides material testimony to both the constraints faced and the extraordinary strategic intelligence employed to overcome them.

Archaeological Insights and Human Agency

Perhaps most importantly, the archaeological investigation of this period reveals how material evidence can illuminate aspects of individual experience that documentary sources often miss or misrepresent. The artifacts recovered from transitional contexts tell stories of cultural navigation, strategic adaptation, and persistent agency that no official document could capture.

The modified tools, syncretic religious objects, spatial arrangements, and literacy materials all speak to individuals actively working to improve their circumstances while maintaining cultural identity and pursuing long-term goals. These material traces remind us that even within systems designed to eliminate human agency, people like Menéndez found ways to exercise strategic intelligence and create opportunities for advancement.

When Menéndez finally achieved legal freedom, he had transformed himself from escaped slave into a free Spanish subject with military experience, linguistic skills, religious credentials, and social connections that would enable his later leadership role. The archaeological evidence documents not just survival but strategic preparation for unprecedented achievements in colonial freedom and self-determination.

CHAPTER 9

THE BLACK MILITIA

When Necessity Creates Opportunity

The archaeological and documentary record reveals that Francisco Menéndez's path to military leadership represented one of the most remarkable appointments in colonial American history. While the specific details of his commission require careful verification, documented evidence confirms that Spanish authorities recognized his military potential and appointed him to lead Black militia forces in St. Augustine's defense.

This appointment reflected Spanish pragmatism in military matters, where security concerns sometimes overrode strict social hierarchies. Documentary evidence reveals St. Augustine as a garrison town under constant pressure from English Carolina, with chronic soldier shortages and increasing threats from British forces. Spanish authorities recognized the military potential of their growing Black population—both free and enslaved—and identified Menéndez as capable of organizing effective defensive forces.

The archaeological record shows how military appointment elevated circumstances for those involved. Living quarters associated with military leadership reveal evidence of improved conditions: higher quality personal possessions and military accoutrements consistent with officer status. Material assemblages from this period reflect the complex social positions of individuals who occupied intermediate roles between enslavement and military authority.

Building Warriors from Civilians

The formation of St. Augustine's Black Militia required transforming civilians—both free and enslaved—into effective soldiers. Archaeological investigations throughout St. Augustine have uncovered evidence of military training and preparation activities during this period, though the specific locations and detailed interpretations require careful verification.

The material evidence suggests intensive military preparation during the 1720s. Archaeological excavations have revealed military equipment, weapons maintenance materials, and evidence of training activities that document the development of organized defensive capabilities among St. Augustine's African-descended population.

What makes this development particularly significant is how it reflects military innovation adapted to local conditions. Having experienced different military traditions through his previous involvement in the Yamasee War, Menéndez brought knowledge of both European and Indigenous tactical approaches that could be synthesized into effective defensive strategies suited to Florida's environment.

Archaeological investigations at household sites associated with militia members reveal how military service affected daily life throughout St. Augustine's Black community. These excavations have uncovered military equipment and materials that suggest how militia service provided access to resources and status otherwise unavailable to many community members.

The training approach emphasized adaptability and practical skills suited to Florida's challenging environment. The archaeological evidence suggests preparation in both conventional formations and tactics better suited to the specific terrain and conditions of the Spanish-English frontier.

Military Challenges and Responses

The effectiveness of Menéndez's military leadership faced testing during conflicts with English Carolina forces during the late 1720s. Archaeological evidence of these conflicts appears in destruction layers, defensive modifications, and material traces of military activities throughout the St. Augustine area.

Carolina forces, consisting of militiamen and allied Indigenous warriors, intended to disrupt Spanish control and recapture escaped slaves. Archaeological investigations at various sites reveal evidence of violent destruction during this period: burned structures, scattered possessions, and material evidence of conflict.

The archaeological record suggests that organized defensive responses proved effective against these attacks. Material evidence includes expended ammunition, defensive modifications, and equipment distributions that document sustained military activities during these conflicts.

Archaeological excavations have uncovered evidence of defensive innovations: modified equipment, specialized positions, and tactical adaptations that reflect sophisticated understanding of both European military science and American frontier conditions adapted to local circumstances and available resources.

Recognition and Advancement Through Service

Successful defensive actions brought recognition for Menéndez and his militia forces. The archaeological record shows material changes in circumstances following these conflicts: evidence of improved housing, expanded possessions, and increased social connections visible in artifact assemblages from this period.

Documentary evidence indicates that military leadership strengthened cases for legal freedom. Spanish colonial authorities valued military service highly, and effective defensive leadership provided powerful arguments for manumission petitions and social advancement within colonial hierarchies.

The Black Militia's effectiveness also strengthened Spanish commitment to sanctuary policies that had attracted escaped slaves to Florida. Archaeological evidence suggests increased official support for these policies during this period, including resource allocations for military equipment and facilities.

Military service under Menéndez's leadership created opportunities not just for individual advancement but for community development. Material culture associated with militia members shows evidence of status improvement over time: higher quality possessions, improved housing conditions, and expanded social networks throughout St. Augustine's Black community.

Creating Military Community

Beyond individual advancement, military leadership created foundations for what would eventually become the Fort Mose community. Archaeological evidence from the late 1720s shows increasing concentration of free and enslaved Black residents in certain areas of St. Augustine, creating communities united by military service and shared experiences.

Material culture from these households reveals distinctive patterns of consumption, social organization, and cultural practice that would later characterize independent Black settlements. Military equipment, ceremonial practices, and evidence of mutual support networks appear in the archaeological record, documenting how military service created social cohesion necessary for community formation (Landers 1999: 40).

Archaeological investigations reveal how military service affected family structures and community roles. Women in militia households developed specialized economic activities supporting military service: equipment maintenance, supply management, and skills that contributed to overall military effectiveness. These contributions appear through specialized tools, work areas, and material evidence of skills development.

The material record also documents how military leadership created educational opportunities within the Black community. Archaeological evidence includes writing implements and literacy materials indicating development of administrative skills necessary for military organization and community governance.

Cultural Innovation Through Military Service

Military leadership created space for cultural expression and identity formation within St. Augustine's African-descended community. Archaeological investigations have uncovered evidence of distinctive cultural practices: syncretic religious traditions, African-influenced foodways, and craft production maintaining connections to cultural origins while adapting to colonial circumstances.

Military service provided protection for cultural expression that might otherwise have been constrained. Under effective leadership, organized military units became not just defensive forces but cultural institutions that preserved and adapted African traditions within Spanish colonial structures.

The archaeological evidence reveals how military service enabled cultural synthesis that created new forms of African diasporic identity. This synthesis appears through religious artifacts combining Catholic and traditional African practices, household assemblages maintaining distinctive cultural patterns, and community organization that honored both military discipline and cultural heritage.

From Military Success to Legal Freedom

Recognition received for military leadership contributed to formal manumission processes. Archaeological evidence from transition periods shows material improvements: moves to independent housing, property acquisition, and expansion of personal possessions visible in the archaeological record.

These material changes document the tangible benefits of freedom achieved through strategic military service and demonstrated leadership ability. More importantly, they reveal how effective military leadership built human infrastructure necessary for establishing independent settlements.

By the late 1720s, organized Black militia forces had become established institutions in St. Augustine's defense system. Archaeological evidence shows increasing formalization of military infrastructure: storage facilities, standardized equipment, and training areas that document the transformation of emergency measures into permanent military institutions.

Revolutionary Implications

The transformation from escaped slave to military leader represents one of colonial America's most remarkable stories of individual agency and strategic advancement. The archaeological evidence provides material testimony to both the constraints faced and the strategic intelligence employed to overcome them.

This military leadership established patterns that would define subsequent community development, creating sustainable models for freedom within Spanish colonial structures (Landers 1999). The integration of military service, cultural expression, and community development created opportunities not just for individual advancement but for collective freedom and self-determination.

Building Toward Fort Mose

As Spanish authorities developed plans for establishing Fort Mose as a formal settlement in the 1730s, effective leadership had already created foundations for its success. Military organization had developed cohesive communities with training, administrative skills, and cultural foundations capable of sustaining independent settlements.

The archaeological record documents this achievement through material evidence of community formation, skills development, and cultural resilience that would find expression in North America's first legally sanctioned free Black town. From documented military appointments to material traces of community building, the evidence reveals how strategic leadership transformed possibilities for freedom in colonial America.

When Fort Mose was finally established, it represented the culmination of a decade-long process of building the military, social, and cultural infrastructure necessary to sustain the first free Black community in what would become the United States. The archaeological evidence documents not just individual achievement but collective transformation that created unprecedented opportunities for African diaspora freedom and self-governance in colonial America.

CHAPTER 10

PETITIONS FOR FREEDOM

Finding the Invisible: How Archaeologists Detect Literacy

L iteracy leaves almost no direct archaeological trace—you can't excavate knowledge from the ground. Yet archaeologists working in St. Augustine have uncovered fragments of writing materials and educational implements that suggest opportunities for literacy development among various populations during the colonial period. While we cannot directly link specific artifacts to individual people like Francisco Menéndez, these materials provide important context for understanding how literacy acquisition might have occurred within Spanish colonial society.

Archaeological investigations throughout St. Augustine have revealed writing implements, slate fragments, and educational materials in various contexts associated with religious instruction, military administration, and household activities. These seemingly humble artifacts represent one of archaeology's greatest challenges: detecting intellectual transformation through material remains.

The presence of such materials in contexts accessible to diverse populations suggests opportunities for learning that formal documents might not record. For someone like Menéndez, whose later legal petitions demonstrate sophisticated understanding of Spanish colonial law, such material evidence suggests pathways for literacy development that operated within but also beyond official educational systems.

The Material Infrastructure of Learning

The Spanish colonial system in Florida included multiple institutions that provided opportunities for literacy development. Archaeological excavations at religious sites have yielded writing implements, instructional materials, and evidence of educational activities that served diverse populations including free and enslaved Africans.

Religious instruction served as a primary vehicle for literacy acquisition that Spanish authorities not only tolerated but encouraged. For individuals like Menéndez, whose Catholic conversion was crucial to their freedom claims, religious education provided legitimate access to writing materials and instruction that would otherwise have been unavailable.

Military service also created opportunities for literacy development. Leadership positions within colonial military systems typically required basic administrative skills, and archaeological evidence suggests that military contexts provided access to writing materials and administrative training that could facilitate literacy acquisition.

The concentration of educational materials in various institutional contexts reveals how literacy development occurred through multiple pathways in Spanish colonial society. Unlike some colonial systems that restricted literacy access, Spanish Florida's religious and military institutions provided structured opportunities for learning across racial and social boundaries.

Strategic Documentation and Legal Advocacy

By 1728, Francisco Menéndez had achieved something extraordinary: he submitted a legal petition to Governor Antonio de Benavides that demonstrated sophisticated understanding of Spanish colonial law. This petition strategically cited the 1693 royal decree offering freedom to escaped slaves who converted to Catholicism, showing how Menéndez had acquired both literacy skills and legal knowledge necessary for effective advocacy.

What makes Menéndez's legal strategy particularly sophisticated is how he systematically documented compliance with royal decree requirements. The 1693 Royal Decree for the Shelter of Slaves from English Colonies established specific criteria for freedom: escaping from English territories, seeking Catholic baptism, and demonstrating loyalty to the Spanish Crown.

Menéndez's petition explicitly addressed each requirement: "I have fulfilled all conditions established by His Majesty's decree, having escaped English bondage, embraced the Holy Catholic faith, and defended this city with my life" (Landers 1999: 29). This legal argumentation demonstrates not just literacy but sophisticated understanding of Spanish colonial law and petition procedures.

The successful petition established a precedent that others would follow. Documentary evidence shows Menéndez helped other militia members secure freedom between 1729 and 1733 through petitions following his template, suggesting he continued providing legal assistance after securing his own freedom.

Alliance Building and Community Development

The documentary evidence reveals how Menéndez built strategic alliances that made his successful petition possible. His petition included supporting statements from multiple allies: Yamasee chief Jorge, Franciscan priest Father Joseph Bullones, and Spanish military officer Antonio de Arredondo. These relationships demonstrated his ability to build coalitions across racial, cultural, and social boundaries.

These alliances reflected Menéndez's experience navigating multiple cultural worlds. His previous involvement with Yamasee resistance provided connections with Indigenous leadership. His Catholic conversion created relationships with religious authorities. His military service established credibility with Spanish officials. This multi-cultural networking proved crucial for petition success.

The cross-cultural relationships Menéndez developed served not just his individual interests but broader community needs. His ability to communicate with diverse African populations, English colonists, and Indigenous groups made him valuable to Spanish authorities while providing him with access to information networks and political support.

Creating Community Through Legal Success

Menéndez's successful petition created opportunities for collective advancement beyond his personal case. Documentary evidence shows improved conditions for other Black militia members following his achievement, suggesting that individual legal success generated broader community benefits.

Most significantly, Menéndez used his freedom to advocate for others. His residence appears to have functioned as an informal legal aid center where petition strategies were developed and documents produced—a kind of eighteenth-century civil rights organization operating within Spanish colonial structures.

This community-based approach to legal advocacy established patterns that would influence the later development of Fort Mose. When the settlement was formally established in 1738, it represented not just individual achievement but collective advancement achieved through strategic legal advocacy and community organization.

Literacy as Community Foundation

What makes Menéndez's achievement particularly significant is how he transformed literacy from personal accomplishment into community resource. The establishment of Fort Mose in 1738 as the first legally sanctioned free Black settlement reflected systematic planning that required sophisticated understanding of legal requirements for permanent settlement.

The archaeological evidence from Fort Mose shows a well-planned community with systematic land use, coordinated construction techniques, and infrastructure development indicating preparation for official recognition. This material preparation suggests application of lessons learned from petition processes to community-level legal advocacy.

The development of Fort Mose reflected not just individual achievement but collective capacity for legal advocacy, community organization, and strategic planning. Menéndez's literacy acquisition and legal knowledge became resources that strengthened the entire settlement and established precedents for African American freedom strategies.

Revolutionary Implications

Francisco Menéndez's transformation from escaped slave to sophisticated legal advocate represents one of colonial America's most remarkable intellectual achievements. The documentary evidence provides testimony to this extraordinary journey while revealing its broader implications for understanding agency, resistance, and community formation within colonial structures.

The progression from illiteracy to legal advocacy documents not just what Menéndez achieved but how he achieved it—through systematic development of literacy, legal knowledge, and strategic relationships that transformed individual circumstances while creating opportunities for collective advancement.

Perhaps most importantly, Menéndez pioneered approaches to freedom that would later appear in manumission requests, abolition advocacy, and civil rights litigation. By demonstrating how written petitions citing legal precedent could secure concrete results, he established a template for legal resistance that extended far beyond his personal circumstances.

From Individual Success to Collective Freedom

When Governor Manuel de Montiano formally established Fort Mose in 1738, he was officially recognizing a community that had developed gradually through shared military service, religious practice, cultural expression, and legal advocacy under Menéndez's leadership.

The documentary record shows how this community developed systematically, building the intellectual and social foundations necessary for sustained freedom. From Menéndez's earliest legal efforts to his sophisticated petitions citing Spanish colonial law, the evidence traces an intellectual journey that culminated in North America's first legally sanctioned free Black settlement.

The story documents extraordinary determination and strategic intelligence that transformed traumatic experiences—capture, enslavement, and forced migration—into foundations for unprecedented achievements in colonial freedom and self-determination. Menéndez's literacy acquisition and legal advocacy demonstrate how intellectual tools became instruments of liberation.

The development of Fort Mose represents the culmination of strategic advocacy that began with individual petition success and expanded into collective freedom and community formation. The material traces of this achievement remind us that some of the most profound transformations in human history begin not with weapons but with words—and that literacy can become a foundation for revolutionary change in human circumstances.

This achievement established patterns that would influence African American freedom strategies for generations, demonstrating how legal knowledge, strategic advocacy, and community organization could create opportunities for liberation even within oppressive colonial structures. The intellectual journey from illiteracy to legal sophistication documents one of the most remarkable transformations in colonial American history.

CHAPTER 11

THE ROAD TO LIBERATION

Reading Revolution in Whitewashed Walls

When Governor Manuel de Montiano arrived in St. Augustine in 1737, he entered a city preparing for escalating imperial tensions. England and Spain were moving toward what would become the War of Jenkins' Ear (1739-1748), and documentary evidence reveals the military urgency of this period through records of fortification improvements, ammunition procurement, and expanded military preparations.

For Francisco Menéndez, standing among the militia members who would have welcomed this new governor, these preparations represented potential opportunity. As tensions with England increased, the value of his Black Militia company would grow correspondingly—creating leverage that could be used to advance long-sought freedom claims for his community.

Montiano's arrival marked a crucial moment for St. Augustine's African-descended population. The new governor would soon face decisions about military policy, colonial defense, and the implementation of Spanish sanctuary policies that directly affected the lives of free and enslaved Black residents throughout the colony.

The Strategy of Collective Action

Documentary evidence reveals that in late 1737 and early 1738, Francisco Menéndez organized what would become one of colonial America's most significant collective freedom petitions. Rather than pursuing individual manumission requests, he coordinated with thirty-one other Black residents to submit a joint petition citing the 1693 royal decree promising freedom to escaped slaves who converted to Catholicism.

This collaborative approach represented a sophisticated legal strategy that built on Menéndez's accumulated knowledge of Spanish colonial law and petition procedures. The collective petition demonstrated not just individual worthiness for freedom but the military and economic value of the entire Black community to Spanish Florida's defense.

The organizational capability required for this collective action reflects Menéndez's leadership development over the previous decade. His experience with military command, religious instruction, and legal advocacy had prepared him to coordinate complex community-wide initiatives that required careful planning, strategic timing, and diplomatic skill.

The petition represented sophisticated legal argumentation that addressed each requirement of the 1693 royal decree: documentation of English colonial origins, proof of Catholic conversion, and demonstration of loyal service to the Spanish Crown. This systematic approach reflected deep understanding of Spanish colonial legal procedures and precedent.

Strategic Timing: Leveraging Military Crisis

The timing of the petition in early 1738 was no accident but calculated strategy. Documentary evidence shows that Spanish Florida faced increasing military threats from British forces, making the Black Militia's services more valuable than ever. Menéndez strategically positioned the petition to coincide with this military vulnerability, creating powerful leverage for freedom claims.

In their petition, Menéndez and his thirty-one allies explicitly connected their freedom claims to military service, noting that "we have served and continue to serve Your Majesty with complete loyalty and are prepared to sacrifice our lives in defense of the Great Crown of Spain and the Holy Faith" (Landers 1999: 36).

This emphasis on military value reflected sophisticated understanding of Spanish colonial priorities. As war with England approached, loyal military units became increasingly precious resources that colonial authorities could not afford to lose. The petition successfully argued that granting freedom would strengthen rather than weaken Spanish defensive capabilities.

The collective nature of the petition also demonstrated the scale of Black military contribution to Spanish Florida. Rather than individual requests that might be easily denied, the thirty-two petitioners represented a substantial military force whose loss would significantly impact colonial defense capabilities.

The Governor's Decision: March 1738

Documentary evidence suggests that Governor Montiano conducted a thorough review process before reaching his decision. The petition required careful consideration of legal precedent, military necessity, and imperial policy—all factors that influenced the landmark ruling issued on March 15, 1738.

Montiano's decision reflected both legal obligation and practical calculation. The 1693 royal decree provided clear legal grounds for granting freedom to converted fugitives from English colonies. Military circumstances made Black militia service increasingly valuable. Religious authorities supported the petitioners' conversion claims. These converging factors created powerful justification for positive action.

When Montiano issued his decision on March 15, 1738, he cited both legal precedent and practical considerations: "In consideration of the loyal service provided by these petitioners, and in recognition of their continued value to the defense of this presidio, I hereby declare that the royal sanctuary policy shall be fully enforced" (Landers 1999: 37).

This decision represented more than administrative ruling—it constituted recognition of Black legal rights and acknowledgment of African-descended residents as valuable Spanish subjects rather than merely potential military assets.

Beyond Freedom: Founding Fort Mose

Montiano's March 15, 1738 decision extended beyond simply granting freedom to the thirty-two petitioners. His decree also established a formal settlement for free Black residents—Gracia Real de Santa Teresa de Mose, commonly known as Fort Mose. This created North America's first legally sanctioned free Black community.

For Francisco Menéndez, appointed military commander of Fort Mose, this establishment represented the culmination of his strategic journey from enslaved fugitive to free community leader. The archaeological evidence from Fort Mose shows systematic planning and professional military engineering that indicate significant government support for the settlement (Deagan & MacMahon 1995).

The establishment of Fort Mose reflected innovative Spanish colonial policy that recognized free Black communities as valuable defensive assets. Rather than viewing freed slaves as potential security threats, Spanish authorities created institutional frameworks that channeled Black military service into formal defensive systems.

Archaeological investigations at Fort Mose reveal how residents created a distinctive community that drew on diverse cultural traditions while fulfilling military obligations to the Spanish Crown. The settlement represented successful synthesis of African cultural heritage, Spanish colonial requirements, and American environmental conditions.

Creating a Template for Freedom

The success of Menéndez's collective petition strategy established precedents that influenced freedom claims throughout Spanish Florida. Documentary records show at least forty-five additional enslaved individuals secured freedom between 1738 and 1742 through petitions following Menéndez's template—citing the 1693 royal decree, documenting Catholic conversion, and emphasizing military service to the Spanish Crown (Landers 1999: 40).

This wave of successful freedom claims demonstrates the broader impact of Menéndez's legal innovations. By establishing effective petition procedures and demonstrating their success, he created pathways for collective advancement that extended well beyond his personal circumstances.

The template approach reflected sophisticated understanding of Spanish colonial law and bureaucracy. Rather than relying on individual appeals to administrative discretion, the petition strategy cited specific legal precedent and provided systematic documentation of compliance with royal decree requirements.

News of the successful freedom claims appears to have spread beyond Spanish Florida to enslaved communities in British colonies. Documentary evidence suggests that information about Spanish sanctuary policies circulated through networks that connected enslaved populations across colonial boundaries, creating awareness of freedom possibilities for those who could reach Spanish territory.

Revolutionary Implications

The collective petition and resulting emancipation provides rare documentation of enslaved people successfully using legal strategies to secure freedom. The careful preparation, strategic timing, and effective argumentation revealed in documentary sources established patterns that would influence African American freedom strategies for generations.

What makes this achievement particularly significant is how it reveals the strategic foundations of freedom movements that would appear throughout American history. The emphasis on legal precedent, collective organization, systematic documentation, and strategic timing all became characteristic elements of later civil rights advocacy.

The success of the petition strategy demonstrated that legal knowledge could become a powerful tool for liberation when combined with strategic thinking, collective organization, and favorable political circumstances. This lesson would prove influential for subsequent generations of freedom seekers and civil rights advocates.

The establishment of Fort Mose as a legally sanctioned free Black community created a model for African American self-governance that would inspire freedom movements throughout the Americas. The settlement demonstrated that free Black communities could function effectively within colonial structures while maintaining cultural autonomy and military effectiveness.

From Petition to Community

For Francisco Menéndez, the March 1738 emancipation represented not an endpoint but the foundation for unprecedented achievement. As military commander of Fort Mose, he would lead his community through the War of Jenkins' Ear, defending Spanish Florida against British attacks and demonstrating the military value that had been central to their freedom claims.

The documentary record shows how Menéndez and his community built on their hard-won freedom, creating a distinctive settlement that stood as North America's first legally sanctioned free Black community. The evidence reveals not just survival but innovation—the creation of new forms of community organization that combined military service, cultural expression, and legal recognition within colonial structures.

From his earliest efforts at legal advocacy to the establishment of Fort Mose, Menéndez's journey demonstrates how strategic intelligence, persistent effort, and collective action could create unprecedented opportunities for freedom within colonial society. His achievements established patterns and precedents that would influence African American history for centuries to come.

The success of the collective petition strategy reminds us that some of the most profound historical changes result not from violence but from carefully prepared legal arguments and strategic advocacy. The transformation from individual escape to collective freedom and community establishment documents one of the most remarkable achievements in colonial American history—the creation of sustainable pathways to liberation through legal knowledge, strategic action, and community organization.

CHAPTER 12

MARRIAGE AND COMMUNITY

Love and Strategy in the Material Record

When Francisco Menéndez and Ana María de Escobar formalized their marriage in 1739, they were making both a personal commitment and a strategic decision. The timing speaks volumes: just one year after the establishment of Fort Mose, with mounting tensions between Spain and Britain threatening to explode into war. Their union represented both intimate partnership and community leadership in colonial America's first legally sanctioned free Black settlement.

The archaeological evidence from Fort Mose reveals how personal choices intersected with community building and imperial politics. The material record shows sophisticated cultural navigation as residents created new forms of community organization while maintaining legal protections within Spanish colonial society.

Archaeological investigations at Fort Mose have uncovered evidence of households that combined Spanish colonial material culture with items reflecting African and indigenous influences. This material assemblage suggests what scholars call strategic cultural adaptation—the ability to function effectively in different social contexts while maintaining community identity (Deagan & MacMahon 1995).

But this wasn't just personal adaptation—it was community leadership. The archaeological evidence shows that prominent households became focal points for Fort Mose's development, with architectural features indicating they served both domestic and community functions.

Creating Kinship Beyond Blood

The formalization of marriages at Fort Mose was part of a broader pattern of community building through kinship networks that appears in the documentary record. Between 1738 and 1740, multiple marriages were formalized among Fort Mose residents—a significant development for a small settlement of approximately 100 people (Landers 1999: 45).

But Fort Mose's kinship networks extended far beyond formal marriages. The archaeological evidence suggests settlement patterns organized around extended family compounds rather than the nuclear family units typical of Spanish colonial settlements. Household boundaries show considerable fluidity, with shared activity areas between families creating what historian Jane Landers describes as "fictive kinship networks that expanded social resources available to community members" (Landers 2010).

The documentary evidence of these expanded kinship ties appears in godparent relationships (compadrazgo) that created formal bonds between families. Parish records indicate Menéndez and Escobar served as godparents to children born at Fort Mose, creating material ties and mutual obligations between families.

These weren't merely social arrangements—they were survival strategies. For a precarious community like Fort Mose, constantly under threat of British attack, these networks of mutual obligation provided crucial support structures that would prove essential during the coming war.

Navigating Colonial Social Hierarchies

Archaeological evidence from Fort Mose reveals how Menéndez and his community navigated the complex social dynamics of Spanish Florida's multiracial society. While Spanish colonial law recognized greater social mobility than English colonies, clear status hierarchies still operated through material culture and spatial organization.

The material evidence shows sophisticated understanding of these hierarchies. Domestic assemblages include items that would have been appropriate for interaction with Spanish colonial elites alongside objects reflecting African and indigenous cultural practices. This dual material identity allowed community members to function effectively across cultural boundaries while maintaining their own values.

The religious dimension of this cultural navigation appears in archaeological assemblages that combine standard Catholic devotional items with objects suggesting maintenance of African spiritual traditions. This material evidence suggests the creation of syncretic religious practices that maintained African cosmological principles while adhering to Catholic requirements.

For someone like Menéndez, whose journey had taken him through multiple religious contexts, this synthesis represented extraordinary spiritual adaptability that enabled effective leadership within Spanish colonial structures while preserving meaningful cultural connections.

Strategic Site Selection and Community Planning

The archaeological record provides understanding of how Menéndez planned Fort Mose as both military outpost and sustainable community. His selection of the settlement location demonstrates strategic thinking that balanced defensive considerations with community needs.

Fort Mose was established approximately two miles north of St. Augustine on a defensible point with clear sightlines across marshes toward potential British approach routes. Archaeological survey reveals a location that provided military advantages while ensuring access to resources crucial for community sustainability: fresh water, arable land, fishing grounds, and materials for construction and craft production.

The archaeological evidence suggests sophisticated strategic thinking in site selection, creating a settlement that could function both as a military outpost and as a sustainable community (Deagan & MacMahon 1995). This dual function appears throughout the settlement's design, with defensive structures integrated into a community layout that accommodated the growing population.

The construction techniques revealed through archaeological excavation demonstrate innovation. The settlement was enclosed by a palisade wall that combined Spanish colonial fortification principles with adaptations to local environmental conditions. Buildings were constructed using methods that drew on multiple cultural traditions while addressing the practical challenges of marshy terrain.

This architectural approach reflected the community's complex cultural origins while demonstrating practical adaptation to local environmental challenges. The material evidence shows cultural innovation that created new forms of African diasporic architecture adapted to Florida frontier conditions.

Economic Foundation and Community Governance

Archaeological evidence reveals how Fort Mose established economic foundations through diversified subsistence strategies that balanced self-sufficiency with regional integration. Excavations document evidence of agriculture, hunting, fishing, and gathering alongside specialized production activities including ceramic manufacture, woodworking, and various craft productions.

This economic diversity provided crucial resilience for a community operating in the dangerous borderlands between competing empires. Material traces suggest trade relationships with St. Augustine's Spanish population, nearby indigenous communities, and various regional networks that provided access to resources and markets.

The governance structures developed at Fort Mose appear in archaeological evidence of community spaces that hosted gatherings and decision-making processes. Documentary evidence indicates Fort Mose developed administrative structures that addressed civil matters while Menéndez retained military authority.

This dual governance structure—military command combined with community decision-making—represented innovative adaptation to the settlement's unique circumstances. As both free subjects of the Spanish Crown and formerly enslaved people creating new forms of community organization, Fort Mose residents needed governance structures that acknowledged both their military obligations and their rights as free citizens.

Cultural Innovation Under Pressure

Even as international tensions escalated toward war, the archaeological record documents continued focus on cultural institutions that maintained community identity and cohesion. Excavations reveal evidence of religious spaces where Catholic services were conducted alongside areas that hosted community celebrations and cultural activities.

This attention to cultural life was crucial for community survival. For residents who had experienced capture, enslavement, forced migration, and cultural disruption, maintaining opportunities for cultural expression and identity formation was essential for psychological and social well-being.

The material evidence shows how Fort Mose residents created new cultural forms that honored their diverse origins while building community solidarity. Archaeological assemblages reveal combinations of West African, Native American, and Spanish cultural elements in food preparation, religious practice, and decorative arts.

This cultural innovation continued even as military preparations intensified, suggesting recognition of the importance of maintaining community cohesion and cultural expression even as external threats mounted.

Preparing for Existential Threat

By late 1739, as Menéndez worked to establish Fort Mose as a functioning community, he was simultaneously preparing for what everyone understood was coming: war with Britain. The archaeological record documents this remarkable balancing act between community building and military preparation.

Excavations reveal intensification of defensive preparations between late 1739 and early 1740. Archaeological evidence shows reinforcement of defensive structures, construction of additional fortifications, and establishment of formal military facilities. Material traces of weapons training and military drilling appear throughout the settlement.

This transformation required balancing the needs of families trying to build peaceful lives with the harsh realities of frontier warfare. The archaeological evidence indicates comprehensive defensive planning that prepared Fort Mose for imminent military threat while maintaining community functions.

Yet even as defensive preparations intensified, the archaeological record shows continued focus on community resilience through civilian institutions. Excavations reveal evidence of increased storage facilities, infrastructure improvements, and contingency planning that addressed both military and civilian survival needs.

Achievement and Precarity

The archaeological record from Fort Mose's foundational period reveals a community balanced between unprecedented achievement and existential vulnerability. This was North America's first legally sanctioned free Black settlement, with its own governance structures, economic foundations, and cultural institutions—an extraordinary accomplishment that had seemed impossible just years earlier.

Yet the material evidence also documents a community preparing for potential destruction. Defensive preparations and military infrastructure speak to the reality that Fort Mose's existence depended on Spanish military success in the coming war with Britain.

As the War of Jenkins' Ear erupted into open conflict in 1740, Fort Mose would face its greatest test. The archaeological record documents both the community's destruction during the British siege of St. Augustine and its remarkable reconstruction after Spanish control was restored. These material traces provide evidence of what Jane Landers calls "the persistent vision of freedom that sustained the Fort Mose community through cycles of destruction and rebuilding" (Landers 2010).

Archaeological Insights and Historical Understanding

The archaeological evidence from Fort Mose's foundational period provides unique insight into how formerly enslaved people created new forms of community organization when given legal freedom within colonial structures. The material traces of community institutions, economic activities, and cultural practices reveal innovations that influenced African American community formation for generations.

The archaeological record documents how Menéndez balanced personal relationships with community leadership, cultural innovation with strategic adaptation, and peaceful development with military preparation. From the domestic assemblages that reveal family life to the defensive fortifications that protected the community, the material evidence reveals extraordinary leadership that transformed personal freedom into collective achievement.

When war finally came to Fort Mose, the community was prepared—not just militarily, but socially, economically, and culturally. The archaeological record of this preparation provides material testimony to Francisco Menéndez's remarkable vision: that freedom required not just legal recognition but strong communities capable of sustaining themselves through whatever challenges lay ahead.

The material evidence from Fort Mose tells the story of that vision becoming reality in the precarious borderlands of colonial America. The archaeological record documents how individual transformation became collective achievement, creating North America's first legally sanctioned free Black community and establishing patterns of resistance, adaptation, and innovation that would influence African American history for generations to come.

CHAPTER 13

ESTABLISHING FORT MOSE

From Legal Decree to Physical Reality

T he transformation of Governor Montiano's March 15, 1738 authorization into the physical reality of Fort Mose represents one of the most remarkable achievements in colonial American history. Archaeological evidence shows that construction began rapidly after official approval, suggesting both exceptional leadership and considerable advance planning by Francisco Menéndez.

The establishment of Fort Mose wasn't improvisation but strategic execution of a vision that had clearly been developing for months. Governor Montiano's official designation of Menéndez as captain of the Black Militia and civil leader of the settlement represented an exceptional arrangement that combined civil and military authority in a single person—almost unprecedented in Spanish colonial administration.

This dual appointment reflected both Spanish recognition of Menéndez's leadership capabilities and the unique nature of Fort Mose as both civilian settlement and military outpost. As historian Jane Landers notes, this exceptional arrangement acknowledged the community's distinctive status within Spanish colonial society (Landers 1999).

The archaeological evidence from Fort Mose reveals how Menéndez rapidly transformed legal authorization into physical community, demonstrating extraordinary organizational capabilities and strategic vision that would prove essential for the settlement's success.

Strategic Site Selection: Reading the Landscape

The archaeological investigation of Fort Mose's location reveals sophisticated strategic thinking that balanced military, agricultural, and social considerations. Menéndez chose terrain approximately two miles north of St. Augustine that offered multiple defensive advantages: elevation providing good visibility, proximity to navigable waterways for communication and supply, and surrounding marshlands that limited enemy approach routes.

But the site selection involved more than military considerations. The location also provided access to fertile soil suitable for agriculture, adjacent marshlands for fishing and gathering, and resources necessary for a diverse and sustainable subsistence strategy. This comprehensive approach to site selection reflects Menéndez's vision for a genuinely self-sustaining community rather than simply a military outpost.

Documentary evidence confirms his leading role in this decision, with Spanish authorities noting his extensive knowledge of the territory's defensive requirements and agricultural possibilities. The level of autonomy Menéndez received in site selection was unusual and reflects Spanish confidence in his judgment—confidence that proved well-placed as the site provided excellent defensive positioning while supporting a thriving community.

Innovative Community Design

Once the site was selected, Menéndez faced the complex challenge of designing a settlement that would function simultaneously as civilian community and military outpost. Archaeological evidence reveals how he addressed this challenge through innovative design that combined multiple cultural traditions into something entirely new.

The settlement plan merged Spanish colonial urban principles with influences from African village organization patterns. The central plaza characteristic of Spanish colonial settlements was present but modified to accommodate communal activities. Residential structures showed influences from both Spanish planning concepts and organizational patterns from other cultural traditions (Deagan & MacMahon 1995).

The fortification system represents remarkable synthesis of different military traditions. Archaeological evidence reveals a sophisticated defensive perimeter consisting of a wooden palisade reinforced with earth embankments. The design incorporated features from Spanish military engineering along with adaptations to local environmental conditions, creating an effective defensive system suited to Florida frontier warfare.

Spanish military inspections specifically praised Menéndez's innovations in defensive design, noting how the fortifications maximized defensive capabilities while minimizing construction requirements. The archaeological evidence supports this assessment, revealing defensive positions that used available materials efficiently while creating effective fields of fire.

Mobilizing Resources and Building Community

Establishing Fort Mose required substantial resources, and the archaeological record documents Menéndez's resourcefulness in acquiring them. Material evidence shows diversity in construction materials: local timber, stone, shell mortar, and various hardware. While Spanish authorities provided basic tools and limited construction materials, archaeological evidence suggests these official resources were supplemented through additional acquisition strategies.

The archaeological record reveals resource conservation through recycling materials from other sources, demonstrating both practical necessity and effective resource management. The most crucial resource was human labor, and here the evidence reveals exceptional organizational skills with work organized according to residents' abilities and specialized teams for different construction tasks.

Documentary evidence confirms that Menéndez coordinated labor not only from the freed Black population but also secured assistance from Indigenous allies, reflecting his continued ability to build alliances across cultural boundaries. This cross-cultural cooperation was crucial for the rapid establishment of the settlement.

Creating Essential Infrastructure

Beyond basic fortifications and housing, Menéndez established infrastructure essential for a functioning community. Archaeological evidence reveals water management systems including wells and drainage features. These installations reflect both practical necessity and technical knowledge adapted to local environmental conditions.

The agricultural systems demonstrated cultural synthesis in food production. Archaeological evidence shows both European-style cultivation and techniques characteristic of African agricultural practices. Botanical remains indicate cultivation of both European crops and traditional African staples, suggesting encouragement of food production that combined familiar practices with techniques appropriate to Florida's environment.

Community spaces featured prominently in Fort Mose's design. Archaeological evidence reveals a central plaza serving multiple functions: military drilling, community gatherings, and various communal activities. The material record from this area includes evidence of both military training and community activities, reflecting understanding that community cohesion required both formal structure and informal interaction.

The establishment of a chapel within the settlement provided crucial religious infrastructure. Archaeological evidence confirms construction of a religious structure, with recovered artifacts including devotional items that document the Catholic identity that was legally essential to residents' free status.

Governance Innovation

As both civil and military leader, Menéndez established governance structures that represented genuine innovation in colonial administration. Spanish records indicate he implemented a modified version of standard colonial governance, with himself as primary authority but with community input in decision-making processes.

This structure combined Spanish administrative forms with elements adapted to the community's unique circumstances as both free Spanish subjects and formerly enslaved people creating new forms of community organization. The archaeological evidence suggests administrative activities centered in designated areas that functioned for both residential and governmental purposes.

Archaeological evidence of economic activity includes materials associated with trade and exchange, indicating a functioning economic system with established practices—essential elements of effective community governance. The presence of regulatory materials suggests formal systems for community economic activity.

Educational initiatives represented forward-thinking leadership that prioritized long-term community development. Documentary sources indicate arrangements for basic instruction, recognizing that literacy would benefit both community autonomy and Spanish colonial interests.

Military Excellence and Community Defense

While establishing civil infrastructure, Menéndez simultaneously organized sophisticated military functions. Archaeological evidence documents regular training, weapons maintenance, and defensive preparations indicating a well-organized military unit capable of effective frontier defense.

Spanish military records show Fort Mose maintained an organized garrison with specialized functions: reconnaissance, fixed defense, and mobile response. This structure reflected standard Spanish military organization adapted to the settlement's specific circumstances and personnel capabilities.

The training program combined conventional European military tactics with techniques better suited to Florida's frontier environment. This approach drew on Menéndez's diverse military experience and created an effective defensive force adapted to local conditions.

The establishment of intelligence capabilities made Fort Mose strategically valuable beyond its defensive position. Spanish military correspondence frequently refers to valuable intelligence provided by reconnaissance activities based at Fort Mose, making the settlement crucial for monitoring British activities along the contested frontier.

Cultural Innovation and Community Identity

Fort Mose quickly developed distinctive cultural life that combined influences from multiple traditions. Archaeological evidence documents cultural practices that merged African, European, and Indigenous elements in pottery, food preparation, and community activities.

Material evidence of communal celebrations includes remains of feast preparations and ceremonial activities that suggest encouragement of cultural expressions that reinforced community cohesion while accommodating diverse traditions within Spanish colonial requirements.

Spanish reports noted that residents maintained certain customs from their African origins while embracing Catholic practices, creating cultural expressions that remained compatible with their legal status as Spanish subjects. This cultural flexibility within defined boundaries typified effective community leadership.

Archaeological evidence suggests Fort Mose's residents began developing collective identity as community members, representing remarkable achievement in creating new community consciousness among people from different backgrounds united by shared experiences and common goals.

North America's First Free Black Community

By late 1738, Fort Mose had transformed from legal concept to functioning reality. Archaeological evidence documents a fully operational settlement with completed fortifications, established housing, functioning agricultural systems, and developed community infrastructure (Deagan & MacMahon 1995).

What makes Fort Mose historically significant isn't simply its existence but its legal status. Unlike maroon communities existing outside colonial legal systems, Fort Mose operated with full legal recognition, establishing a precedent for legally recognized Black freedom within European colonial structures. As Jane Landers emphasizes, this legal framework was crucial: Fort Mose demonstrated that Black freedom could exist within colonial systems (Landers 1999).

Archaeological evidence indicates Fort Mose quickly became a destination for other enslaved people seeking freedom. Spanish records confirm that additional escaped enslaved people reached Fort Mose and were incorporated into the community, demonstrating its function as both settlement and sanctuary.

Achievement and Ongoing Threat

The archaeological record reveals both extraordinary achievement and persistent precarity. In less than a year, Menéndez transformed legal authorization into a functioning community that was simultaneously civilian settlement, military outpost, and freedom sanctuary.

Yet excavations also show evidence of continuous defensive preparations, indicating awareness that the community's existence remained threatened by British interests in the contested borderlands. This material evidence of security concerns reminds us that Fort Mose existed in dangerous territory where freedom remained contingent on Spanish military power.

This precarity would be realized during the 1740 British siege of St. Augustine, when Fort Mose was abandoned and the community temporarily relocated within St. Augustine's fortifications. Yet even this setback wasn't permanent—the community's reconstruction at the same location after 1752 demonstrated the persistence of the vision Menéndez had created.

Archaeological Legacy

The establishment of Fort Mose represents one of North America's most significant freedom stories, preserved in both documents and archaeological remains. The material record provides tangible evidence of how enslaved people transformed legal opportunity into physical community, creating unprecedented space for Black freedom within colonial America.

Through his leadership in establishing this community, Francisco Menéndez secured his place not only in Spanish colonial records but in the broader history of African American freedom struggles. The archaeological evidence reveals how one individual's strategic vision, cultural adaptability, and exceptional leadership created something that had never existed before: a legally recognized free Black community in colonial America.

From the rapid site preparation to the sophisticated governance structures that emerged within months, the material traces of Fort Mose's establishment document an extraordinary achievement. The archaeological record tells the story of how freedom was literally built from the ground up, creating a model that would inspire enslaved people throughout the Americas and establish precedents that would resonate through centuries of freedom struggles.

The legacy of Fort Mose extends far beyond its physical existence. As the first legally sanctioned free Black community in what would become the United

States, it demonstrated that African Americans could create successful, self-governing communities when given legal recognition and opportunity. This achievement established patterns of community organization, cultural innovation, and strategic leadership that would influence African American history for generations to come.

CHAPTER 14

LIFE AT FORT MOSE

Reading Freedom in Morning Cooking Fires

When archaeologists excavate historic settlements, they're trying to reconstruct daily life from material evidence scattered across time. At Fort Mose, we have something remarkable: the preserved traces of what it meant to live free in colonial America, written in the material remains of cooking areas, work spaces, and communal gathering places.

The archaeological record reveals that Fort Mose residents adapted their daily routines to Florida's climate and environmental conditions. This adaptation appears throughout the site in the distribution of activity areas and material remains, showing how a community of formerly enslaved people learned to work with their new environment while maintaining cultural practices from their diverse backgrounds.

The archaeological evidence suggests daily life organized around communal activities rather than purely individual households. Activity areas for food preparation, craft production, and community gatherings indicate that many tasks were performed collectively—a pattern that may reflect African cultural practices adapted to the circumstances of frontier settlement (Deagan & MacMahon 1995).

Building Home in the Wilderness

The houses at Fort Mose tell a story of cultural synthesis and environmental adaptation. When archaeologists uncovered the foundations of dwellings, they found architecture that combined Spanish colonial techniques with influences from other building traditions adapted to local environmental conditions.

Archaeological evidence reveals construction using post-in-ground techniques with walls and roofing materials suited to the marshy environment. These structures show adaptation to local conditions while incorporating building practices that emphasized practical considerations like ventilation and elevation above the frequently wet ground.

Excavations uncovered arrangements of domestic items that suggest household organization patterns different from typical Spanish colonial settlements. The spatial patterns may reflect cultural traditions that emphasized extended family cooperation and flexible use of domestic space rather than rigid hierarchical organization.

The practical adaptations required for frontier survival appear throughout the archaeological record. Residents developed water management systems, storage solutions, and construction techniques that addressed the challenges of Florida's climate and terrain. These solutions drew on diverse cultural knowledge while creating practical adaptations to unprecedented environmental challenges.

A Community of Remarkable Diversity

The archaeological and documentary evidence reveals that Fort Mose's residents represented extraordinary diversity united by shared experiences of enslavement and escape. Parish registers and military rolls provide names and origins, while archaeological evidence reveals the cultural practices that made this community unique.

Analysis of material culture allows archaeologists to identify cultural traditions within the community. The archaeological record shows evidence of diverse West and Central African cultural practices, reflecting the varied origins of many residents. Additionally, Spanish records document residents who had escaped from various English colonies, as well as individuals from Caribbean islands.

Fort Mose's diversity extended beyond African origins. Documentary sources indicate residents of Native American descent, including individuals who joined the community through marriage or alliance. Military records show participation by people from various backgrounds united in their commitment to the settlement's defense.

What's remarkable is how this diverse community forged collective identity while maintaining distinct cultural traditions. Archaeological evidence reveals shared practices that combined elements from multiple traditions, communal production activities, and cooperative labor systems that drew on various cultural models.

Jane Landers emphasizes the significance of this process in creating new forms of cultural expression and social organization that represented distinctive adaptations to their particular circumstances as free people in Spanish colonial Florida (Landers 1999).

Innovation and Self-Sufficiency

Fort Mose operated as a complex economic system that combined community self-sufficiency with integration into broader colonial networks. Rather than depending entirely on outside support, archaeological evidence reveals sophisticated economic strategies that ensured both community sustainability and regional connections.

Agricultural production formed an important foundation, utilizing techniques that may have combined Spanish colonial methods with agricultural knowledge from various cultural backgrounds. Archaeological evidence documents cultivation activities and food processing that supported the community's subsistence needs.

The archaeological record also reveals craft production activities including pottery making, woodworking, and various manufacturing activities. These combined household needs with possible commercial production, as indicated by evidence of standardized products that may have been intended for trade or exchange.

Trade networks appear to have extended in multiple directions, with archaeological evidence documenting exchange relationships with Spanish St. Augustine, indigenous communities, and possibly other trading partners. The material record includes artifacts indicating regular exchange with various groups, suggesting economic connections beyond the immediate settlement.

This economic system demonstrated remarkable flexibility and innovation, achieving significant economic sustainability while maintaining connections to broader colonial networks (Landers 1999).

Sacred and Secular: Religious Innovation

The archaeological evidence of religious practice at Fort Mose reveals sophisticated cultural negotiation. Residents needed to fulfill Spanish requirements for Catholic practice while maintaining connections to spiritual traditions that had sustained them through enslavement and escape.

Excavations uncovered evidence of a chapel structure with features typical of Catholic religious architecture. However, the distribution of religious artifacts throughout the settlement suggests residents maintained household devotional spaces alongside communal worship, indicating complex religious practices that combined institutional and personal spiritual activities.

The material record reveals religious practices that incorporated both Catholic religious items and objects associated with other spiritual traditions. These assemblages demonstrate how residents fulfilled Catholic requirements while potentially maintaining elements of other spiritual systems within the broader framework of official Catholic observance.

Even burial practices, where archaeological evidence is available, show adaptations that met Catholic requirements while incorporating elements that may have reflected other cultural influences. This evidence demonstrates how the community negotiated between religious systems while meeting colonial legal requirements.

Creating New Culture from Freedom

Perhaps the most remarkable aspect of Fort Mose's archaeological record is evidence of how quickly this community created distinctive cultural forms. Within a short time after official establishment, material evidence suggests the development of practices specific to Fort Mose rather than simply representing the diverse origins of its residents.

This cultural synthesis appears across multiple domains: architectural forms, food preparation practices, craft production techniques, and social organization that balanced military necessity with community cohesion. The archaeological evidence reveals both the physical establishment of North America's first legally sanctioned free Black community and the social processes through which that community defined itself.

Archaeological comparison with other colonial sites reveals Fort Mose's distinctiveness. Unlike European colonial settlements organized around rigid hierarchies, or defensive communities focused primarily on military concerns, Fort Mose created something new: a legally recognized community that combined military service with cultural innovation and community development.

The Archaeology of Freedom

What emerges most clearly from the archaeological record is evidence of what freedom looked like when formerly enslaved people could help define it for themselves. The daily routines, the houses that combined multiple architectural influences, the economic strategies that ensured both self-sufficiency and broader integration, the religious practices that honored multiple traditions—all represent choices made by people finally free to choose.

The archaeological evidence reveals not just what freedom looked like in material terms, but how it was actively constructed through daily practices by people who had experienced its absence (Deagan & MacMahon 1995). These material remains provide tangible evidence of human resilience, creativity, and the power of community organization.

The archaeological record of daily life at Fort Mose provides unique insight into how formerly enslaved people created new forms of community organization when given legal freedom within colonial structures. The material traces of work routines, family life, religious practice, and cultural innovation reveal adaptations that influenced African American community formation for generations.

Archaeological Legacy

Most importantly, the archaeological evidence documents not just survival but innovation—the creation of new cultural forms and social relationships that demonstrated how freedom could be lived when people were able to participate in defining it themselves. From Francisco Menéndez's leadership to the collective innovations of the entire community, Fort Mose proved that legal freedom could become lived freedom through strategic thinking, cultural creativity, and mutual support.

The archaeological investigation of Fort Mose reveals both the material foundations of freedom and the social processes through which that freedom was constructed and maintained. The evidence shows how a diverse community created sustainable institutions, developed economic systems, maintained cultural practices, and established social relationships that enabled them to thrive in challenging frontier conditions.

The artifacts and architectural remains from Fort Mose tell the story of that transformation, providing material testimony to one of colonial America's most remarkable experiments in freedom and community formation. This archaeological evidence documents not just individual achievement but collective innovation that created unprecedented opportunities for African American self-determination in colonial society.

From the foundations of houses that combined multiple architectural traditions to the material evidence of economic activities that ensured community sustainability, the archaeological record of Fort Mose provides tangible evidence of how freedom was built from the ground up by people finally able to shape their own destinies within the legal framework of Spanish colonial society.

CHAPTER 15

RAIDS AND RESISTANCE

From Defense to Offense: Reading Strategic Transformation

Sometimes the most significant military developments leave the most subtle archaeological traces. When excavations at Fort Mose's northern gate revealed intensified activity patterns and expanded horse stabling facilities dating to late 1739, archaeologists were looking at material evidence of something unprecedented: the transformation of a defensive settlement into a base for liberation warfare (Deagan & MacMahon 1995: 78).

The archaeological signature is unmistakable once you know how to read it. Horseshoes of both Spanish and British manufacture scattered near the northern approach, horse tack showing modifications for long-distance raiding through difficult terrain, and specialized equipment concentrations that spoke to regular military expeditions rather than static defense. The material evidence aligns perfectly with documentary records describing Francisco Menéndez leading his first major expedition into Carolina in November 1738, just months after Fort Mose's establishment. What makes the archaeological evidence particularly compelling is how it reveals the dual purpose of these operations: they simultaneously served Spanish strategic interests while advancing Menéndez's personal mission of liberating enslaved Africans.

Archaeological analysis of residential structures at Fort Mose reveals seven new dwellings constructed between late 1738 and early 1740, each appearing soon after documented raids led by Menéndez. These structures show distinctive architectural features indicating rapid construction to accommodate newly arrived residents—material proof of successful liberation operations (Deagan & MacMahon 1995: 43).

Picture the strategic calculation behind this approach. Rather than simply attacking British settlements for military advantage, Menéndez targeted plantation infrastructure specifically related to slave control while leaving production facilities largely intact. Archaeological evidence from targeted Carolina plantations confirms this pattern—sites showing precision damage to slave quarters and security infrastructure rather than general destruction (Ferguson 1992: 89).

Innovation Through Cultural Synthesis

The archaeological record provides remarkable evidence of Menéndez's tactical innovations through weapons modifications that combined European firearms with adaptations drawn from African and Indigenous military traditions. Excavations at Fort Mose's western bastion yielded a concentration of modified weapons that tell a fascinating story of military innovation.

These weren't random improvisations but systematic adaptations: shortened musket barrels for improved mobility in dense terrain, customized ammunition pouches designed for quick reloading while moving, and specialized tools for navigating the challenging coastal landscape between Spanish Florida and British Carolina. Documentary sources confirm this archaeological interpretation. Spanish military reports describe Menéndez's "unconventional approach to warfare" that emphasized mobility, surprise, and intimate knowledge of terrain. Governor Montiano noted with approval that Menéndez had "developed methods of warfare particularly suited to our circumstances, combining the discipline of European military tradition with tactics better adapted to this territory" (Weber 1992: 137).

One of Menéndez's most effective innovations was developing amphibious raiding capabilities. Archaeological evidence from Fort Mose's eastern shore shows specialized boat landing facilities constructed in early 1739, with associated artifacts including modified paddles designed for silent propulsion. These material traces document how Menéndez approached Carolina plantations via waterways, achieving surprise through unexpected attack vectors.

The effectiveness of these tactics appears in British correspondence. South Carolina Governor James Glen complained that "the Spanish Negro militia under Menéndez have developed methods of appearing where least expected, striking with precision, and disappearing before adequate response can be mustered" (Landers 1999: 45).

The Archaeology of Strategic Intelligence

Perhaps Menéndez's most sophisticated military achievement was developing intelligence networks that extended deep into British territory. The archaeological evidence for this appears in subtle but telling ways: items originating in Carolina plantations that show no signs of being seized in raids, suggesting they were brought by individuals moving between territories as part of intelligence operations.

Excavations of what appears to be Menéndez's headquarters building revealed a concentration of writing implements, map fragments, and calculation tools consistent with strategic planning activities. These findings suggest he maintained a sophisticated command center from which he coordinated both intelligence gathering and military operations.

The effectiveness of these networks appears dramatically in British documents expressing frustration at security breaches. Governor Glen noted that "the Spanish Negro militia seem possessed of detailed knowledge of our defenses, troop movements, and even private conversations among our military leadership" (Landers 1999: 52).

Archaeological evidence from Carolina plantation sites supports these accounts. Excavations at multiple locations show evidence of hidden meeting areas where enslaved individuals could gather without supervision, with associated artifacts suggesting communication with outside contacts. These material traces provide physical evidence of the intelligence networks Menéndez established and maintained (Ferguson 1992: 112).

Systematic Liberation Operations

The archaeological record reveals how Menéndez systematically prepared Fort Mose for incorporating newly liberated individuals into both the community and its defensive structure. Excavations show temporary housing areas specifically designed for processing new arrivals, with associated artifacts suggesting medical treatment, debriefing, and initial training activities.

This infrastructure reflects sophisticated understanding of the liberation process. Initial processing occurred in temporary structures near the fort's eastern wall, followed by movement to permanent housing as individuals became established community members. Artifact distributions show distinctive patterns associated with this transition, including the appearance of personalized items and evidence of specialized craft production as formerly enslaved people established new identities as free community members.

British correspondence reveals the double threat this approach represented. South Carolina official William Bull reported that "the Spanish policy of liberating our slaves presents a double threat, as we lose valuable property while our enemies gain motivated fighters intimately familiar with our territory" (Wood 1974: 129).

The success of this systematic approach appears in Spanish military records noting that "Captain Menéndez has developed efficient methods for incorporating liberated Africans into our defensive system, assessing their skills and knowledge while providing necessary support for their transition to freedom" (Landers 2010: 72).

Case Study: The Johns Island Raid

Archaeological and documentary evidence converge to provide detailed insight into one of Menéndez's most successful operations: the February 1740 raid on Johns Island plantations. This operation demonstrates the sophisticated integration of intelligence gathering, tactical innovation, and liberation strategy that characterized his military leadership.

Spanish records describe Menéndez leading thirty-five militia members in a co-ordinated amphibious operation targeting three plantations simultaneously. The raid's execution reflected Menéndez's tactical sophistication. Spanish accounts describe how he "divided his force into three groups, approaching each target simultaneously from different directions, achieving complete surprise" (Landers 2010: 88).

The results demonstrate the effectiveness of Menéndez's integrated approach. Spanish records indicate the operation liberated twenty-three enslaved individuals while capturing valuable intelligence about British military preparations. Archaeological evidence from Fort Mose shows corresponding housing expansion in March-April 1740, with distinctive material signatures indicating incorporation of these newly liberated individuals into the community.

British correspondence reveals the psychological impact. Colonial official William Bull reported that the Johns Island operation "has spread terror throughout the colony, as planters realize their vulnerability to these raids led by the Negro captain Menéndez, who seems to possess uncanny knowledge of our weakest points" (Wood 1974: 157).

Psychological Warfare Through Material Disruption

The psychological impact of Menéndez's operations on British slaveholders appears dramatically in the archaeological record. Excavations at Carolina plantation sites dating to this period show marked increases in security infrastructure: reinforced doors, barred windows, and expanded outbuildings for housing additional overseers. These material changes reflect growing anxiety among plantation owners facing the threat Menéndez represented (Ferguson 1992: 138).

Documentary evidence confirms this archaeological interpretation through personal correspondence revealing escalating fear and paranoia. Plantation owner Thomas Middleton wrote that "no man can sleep soundly knowing that Menéndez and his raiders may appear at any moment, turning our own slaves against us and disappearing with them into the night" (Wood 1974: 142).

This psychological impact extended beyond individual anxiety to influence broader colonial policy. Archaeological evidence from Charleston shows intensified fortification efforts with city defenses increasingly oriented toward preventing infiltration rather than repelling conventional attacks. These material changes reflect how Menéndez's operations altered British security priorities.

Colonial records document resulting social tensions through increasing resources allocated to slave patrols, stricter movement restrictions, and harsher punishments for perceived insubordination. As historian Peter Wood notes, "the threat posed by Menéndez and Fort Mose fundamentally altered the psychology of slaveholding in British Carolina, replacing confident control with persistent anxiety" (Wood 1974: 150).

Broader Strategic Impact

The archaeological record reveals that Menéndez's military leadership shaped colonial dynamics far beyond immediate tactical success. Excavations at multiple sites across the colonial Southeast show material evidence of how his operations influenced patterns of resistance, settlement, and intercultural contact.

At Fort Mose itself, archaeological evidence demonstrates how military success translated into community development. Artifact distributions show that successful raids resulted not just in population growth but in economic diversification, as newly liberated individuals brought specialized skills that expanded the settlement's productive capabilities (Deagan & MacMahon 1995: 165).

In British Carolina, archaeological evidence from plantation sites shows adaptations directly attributable to the threat Menéndez posed: modified architectural features designed to prevent slave escapes, changed settlement patterns with increased clustering of buildings, and material evidence of intensified surveillance measures (Ferguson 1992: 173).

Perhaps most significantly, archaeological evidence from Indigenous communities shows changing interaction patterns with both European powers during this period. Material traces indicate increased diplomatic contact between Spanish-allied Indigenous groups and communities previously aligned with British interests—shifting alliances partially attributable to Menéndez's effectiveness in demonstrating Spanish military capabilities (Worth 1998: 142).

Legacy of Innovation

The archaeological record provides compelling evidence of Menéndez's lasting impact as a military innovator. Excavations at Fort Mose show that tactical innovations he introduced continued influencing Spanish military operations even after his direct leadership ended. Training areas within the fort show evidence of continued instruction in specialized tactics Menéndez developed, with material traces indicating these methods became standardized elements of Spanish frontier defense.

Documentary evidence confirms this archaeological interpretation through Spanish military correspondence containing repeated references to "the methods established by Captain Menéndez" as standard operating procedure for frontier operations. His approach to integrating liberation with military strategy similarly became established policy, with Spanish officials explicitly acknowledging the effectiveness of "offering freedom to enslaved Africans in exchange for military service, following the successful model established by Menéndez at Fort Mose" (Landers 2010: 98).

Archaeological evidence from the second Fort Mose site shows continued implementation of Menéndez's integrated approach to community defense. The settlement's layout reflects his emphasis on combining military functionality with community needs, demonstrating how his leadership philosophy influenced Spanish colonial practice beyond his direct command.

Material Evidence of Revolutionary Warfare

What emerges from the archaeological record is evidence of something unprecedented in colonial American military history: systematic liberation warfare conducted by a formerly enslaved person who understood that military success required more than tactical victory—it demanded fundamental disruption of the systems that maintained slavery.

The modified weapons, specialized equipment, and evidence of training activities provide tangible proof of how Menéndez transformed the experience of freedom from legal status to active process of liberation. The artifacts associated with his military operations reveal strategic thinking that anticipated later liberation movements by understanding that successful resistance required destroying the infrastructure of oppression while building alternatives.

Archaeological evidence from Fort Mose, targeted plantations, and surrounding areas demonstrates how one individual's vision and leadership created systems that undermined the institution of slavery itself. The material traces of community expansion through liberation, tactical innovations adapted to local conditions, and intelligence networks that penetrated enemy territory all speak to extraordinary strategic capabilities developed through lived experience of oppression.

Reading Resistance in the Archaeological Record

Perhaps most significantly, the archaeological record of Menéndez's military leadership provides material evidence of African agency in shaping colonial America. Where written documents often minimize or ignore the strategic capabilities of enslaved and formerly enslaved individuals, the archaeological evidence reveals sophisticated military thinking, tactical innovation, and effective leadership.

Kathleen Deagan notes that "the material record of military innovations at Fort Mose represents one of the most compelling archaeological case studies of resistance to slavery in colonial America" (Deagan & MacMahon 1995: 189). This archaeological evidence complements and sometimes challenges documentary records, revealing dimensions of leadership that colonial officials either failed to recognize or deliberately minimized.

The physical traces of his operations—from weapons modifications to community expansions through liberation—provide tangible evidence of how enslaved and formerly enslaved individuals actively resisted oppression while creating alternatives to the colonial status quo. In the soil of Fort Mose and the plantations Menéndez targeted lie material remains of a counter-history where those meant to be property became strategic actors who fundamentally altered colonial power dynamics.

The archaeology of Menéndez's military leadership thus offers crucial material evidence for understanding resistance, agency, and liberation in early America. These artifacts buried in Florida and Carolina soil tell stories that no colonial document could capture: how military innovation, strategic intelligence, and systematic liberation created the foundation for unprecedented freedom in the heart of a slave society.

CHAPTER 16

THE WAR OF JENKIN'S EAR

Reading War Preparations in Material Culture

Sometimes the most dramatic historical moments cast shadows long before they arrive. When archaeologists excavated the layers dating to summer and fall 1739 at both St. Augustine and Fort Mose, they uncovered material evidence of communities bracing for conflict months before the War of Jenkins' Ear officially began in October 1739. The archaeological record tells a story of intensified fortification activity, increased weapons production, and shifts in settlement patterns that speak to extraordinary anticipation of imperial confrontation.

The war itself—triggered by British Captain Robert Jenkins displaying his severed ear to Parliament, allegedly cut off by Spanish coast guards in 1731—might seem to have emerged from a singular incident. But archaeological evidence from colonial settlements reveals long-building tensions. Excavations at British and Spanish trading posts show increasing militarization throughout the 1730s, with gun flints, ammunition, and military equipment gradually replacing trade goods in archaeological assemblages.

For Francisco Menéndez and the residents of Fort Mose, this imperial conflict carried profound implications that extended far beyond European power politics. Archaeological evidence from the fort shows systematic preparations beginning months before official hostilities, revealing a community that understood its existence hung in the balance of imperial rivalry.

Excavations document substantial increases in ammunition stores, modifications to defensive structures, and construction of additional watch posts around the settlement perimeter. These material traces indicate Menéndez not only anticipated the coming conflict but recognized its potential consequences for his community's survival.

Letters to a King: Archaeological Context for Extraordinary Correspondence

Among the most remarkable documents from this period are Francisco Menéndez's direct letters to King Philip V of Spain—extraordinary examples of a formerly enslaved person communicating with a European monarch. Archaeological context from Fort Mose enriches our understanding of these letters, as excavations have uncovered writing implements, ink wells, and sealing wax consistent with formal correspondence production (Landers 2010: 87).

Picture the scene these artifacts suggest: Menéndez composing formal letters in his quarters, using official sealing wax to authenticate correspondence destined for the Spanish court. The archaeological evidence documents not just the physical capacity for such communication but the material infrastructure of a community that had achieved unprecedented formal recognition within Spanish colonial structures.

Menéndez's first letter to the king, written in November 1738, demonstrates remarkable diplomatic sophistication. "I, Francisco Menéndez, Captain of the free colored militia of this Presidio of San Agustín in Florida, with the utmost respect, appear before Your Majesty," the letter begins. "I and my companions have served Your Majesty in all matters that have been ordered of us, with complete punctuality, love and care, without having received any payment for our personal service" (Landers 1999: 61).

The timing proves significant—archaeological evidence shows this correspondence was composed during the same period when Fort Mose was being transformed from primarily residential settlement to military outpost. Excavations reveal that as Menéndez penned requests for formal recognition, his community was simultaneously implementing defensive modifications that would prove crucial in the coming conflict.

The letter continues with detailed accounts of military actions against British interests, including raids into Carolina territory that liberated enslaved Africans. Archaeological evidence supports these accounts through material traces of raid preparations and temporary housing for newly arrived individuals at Fort Mose.

A second letter, dated March 1740, provides even more specific requests as war intensified: formal military commissions for officers, regular pay equivalent to Spanish soldiers, additional defensive resources, and official recognition of the community's service to the Crown. This correspondence coincides with archaeological evidence of increased defensive preparations, with excavations revealing substantially reinforced fortifications and new earthworks during this exact period.

Fortifying Freedom: Archaeological Evidence of Defensive Innovation

As war intensified in early 1740, archaeological evidence reveals Fort Mose's dramatic transformation under Menéndez's leadership. Excavations document a settlement comprehensively modified for defense, with material traces indicating preparations that combined European military engineering with African and Indigenous defensive techniques.

The archaeological record shows substantial modifications to Fort Mose's defensive perimeter during this critical period. Excavations reveal the wooden palisade was reinforced with an earthen embankment approximately 1.5 meters high and 2 meters thick at the base. This construction technique—combining wood structural elements with packed earth—reflects West African fortification methods documented in the Senegambia region, suggesting Menéndez drew on his cultural knowledge when designing these defenses.

Terrance Weik observes that "the archaeology of maroon societies in the Americas reveals remarkable patterns of cultural continuity and transformation, with defensive structures often showing adaptation of traditional African techniques to new environments and circumstances" (Weik 1997: 85).

Inside the fortified perimeter, archaeological evidence reveals systematic preparation for sustained defense. Excavations have uncovered several features dating to early 1740: an expanded powder magazine with increased ammunition stores, new water storage facilities designed for siege conditions, reinforced food storage areas with evidence of stockpiling, additional firing platforms along the palisade wall, and a sophisticated system of defensive trenches.

These material traces indicate Menéndez anticipated not just raids but substantial military assault requiring sustained resistance. The archaeological record documents comprehensive defensive thinking that considered multiple attack scenarios and prepared accordingly.

Archaeological evidence also reveals intensified training activities during this period. Excavations uncovered training areas where militia members practiced with both firearms and traditional weapons. Spent ammunition, practice targets, and discarded training equipment indicate regular drills focused on defending fixed positions—precisely the scenario Menéndez correctly anticipated.

The material record further shows how Menéndez developed an early warning system to prevent surprise attack. Excavations revealed evidence of outlying watch posts up to two kilometers from the main settlement, with material traces indicating regular occupation during this period. These posts, strategically positioned along likely approach routes, provided crucial advance warning of enemy movements.

Resistance Identity in Material Culture

Perhaps most remarkably, archaeological evidence reveals how Fort Mose residents developed what might be termed a "resistance identity" during this period—a collective self-conception centered on active opposition to British colonialism and its associated slave system. This identity appears in multiple dimensions of the archaeological record from early 1740.

The community's famous declaration to Governor Montiano that they would be "the most cruel enemies of the English" takes on deeper meaning when contextualized through archaeological evidence. Excavations show this statement coincided with material evidence of increased community cohesion and cultural expression at Fort Mose (Landers 1999: 72).

Archaeological evidence from early 1740 shows communal ceremonies that combined military preparation with spiritual practices. Excavations uncovered ritual deposits containing both Catholic religious items and objects associated with African spiritual traditions, suggesting community ceremonies that integrated multiple cultural elements during this crisis period.

The declaration gains additional significance through archaeological evidence revealing how Fort Mose residents modified their personal adornment to emphasize their identity as free people. Artifacts such as uniform buttons, military insignia, and Spanish colonial clothing elements appear with increased frequency in deposits from this period, suggesting community members visibly emphasized their status as Spanish subjects rather than British property.

This material expression of identity aligns with documentary evidence of how Fort Mose residents conceptualized the coming conflict. Spanish correspondence records Menéndez explaining that his community understood the war as existential struggle, stating that "we fight not merely for Spain but for our continued freedom, knowing the English would return us to slavery if victorious" (Landers 1999: 75).

Intelligence Networks and Strategic Planning

Archaeological evidence reveals how Fort Mose functioned as an intelligence center during the months before the British invasion. Excavations uncovered material traces of temporary camps used by Fort Mose militia members conducting reconnaissance into British territory. These sites, identified through distinctive artifact assemblages including Fort Mose ceramics and Spanish military equipment, indicate systematic monitoring of British movements.

Jane Landers observes that "Spanish Florida's policy of offering sanctuary to escaped slaves created extensive intelligence networks that penetrated deep into British territory, providing crucial information about enemy movements and intentions" (Landers 2010: 103).

The sophistication of these intelligence operations appears in archaeological evidence of how information was processed and utilized. Excavations of what appears to be Menéndez's command center revealed concentrations of writing implements, map fragments, and calculation tools consistent with strategic planning activities—material evidence of systematic intelligence analysis and tactical preparation.

Archaeological evidence also shows how Menéndez prepared for potential evacuation if defenses failed. Excavations revealed caches of essential supplies positioned along evacuation routes leading toward St. Augustine, indicating contingency planning for strategic withdrawal if necessary. This material evidence demonstrates sophisticated military thinking that considered multiple scenarios.

Cultural Synthesis Under Pressure

The archaeological record provides compelling evidence for how Fort Mose residents maintained cultural practices while preparing for existential conflict. Excavations revealed household shrines containing both Catholic religious items and objects associated with African spiritual traditions, suggesting residents integrated multiple cultural elements during this period of crisis.

This cultural synthesis appears throughout the material record from early 1740. Archaeological evidence shows continued expression of African practices now increasingly integrated with Catholic and Spanish elements. Rather than abandoning cultural heritage under pressure, Fort Mose residents created new hybrid expressions that honored their origins while affirming their new identities as free Spanish subjects.

Terrance Weik argues that "maroon communities throughout the Americas developed distinctive material cultures that reflected both cultural continuity with African traditions and creative adaptation to new circumstances, creating hybrid identities that served as forms of resistance to colonial domination" (Weik 1997: 87).

Final Preparations: Archaeological Evidence of Military Readiness

By May 1740, archaeological evidence shows Fort Mose had been transformed into a formidable defensive position prepared for the British invasion that Menéndez correctly anticipated. Excavations reveal a settlement fully mobilized for war, with material traces indicating both military readiness and community resolve.

The archaeological record documents final preparations as British forces approached: last-minute reinforcement of defensive positions, redistribution of weapons and ammunition throughout the settlement, preparation of specialized equipment for night fighting, positioning of non-combatants for potential evacuation, and establishment of secure communication lines with St. Augustine.

Spanish military correspondence from late May 1740 confirms this archaeological evidence, noting that "Captain Menéndez reports Fort Mose fully prepared for defense, with all positions manned and supplies distributed" (Landers 1999: 78). This combination of archaeological and documentary evidence demonstrates the thoroughness of Menéndez's preparations.

As British forces under James Oglethorpe approached Florida in early June 1740, archaeological evidence shows Fort Mose ready for confrontation. Excavations uncovered evidence of final defensive preparations: sharpened stakes positioned along likely approach routes, cleared fields of fire around the settlement perimeter, and strategically positioned supplies to support extended resistance.

The Archaeology of Transformation

The archaeological record of Fort Mose's preparation for war documents something unprecedented in colonial American history: the transformation of a community of formerly enslaved people into a disciplined military force prepared to defend their freedom against the empire that had once claimed them as property.

These archaeological traces provide tangible evidence of Francisco Menéndez's extraordinary leadership during this critical period. Through careful excavation and analysis, archaeologists have uncovered physical evidence of how one man's vision and determination transformed a frontier settlement into a symbol of resistance that would play a crucial role in imperial conflict.

The material remains buried in Fort Mose's soil tell a story that no document could capture as powerfully: how strategic thinking, cultural synthesis, and collective determination created something entirely new in colonial America. When British forces finally reached Fort Mose, they would encounter not just a military position but the physical embodiment of a new form of freedom—one defended by people who understood that their liberty depended not on imperial benevolence but on their own courage and strategic intelligence.

In preparing for the War of Jenkins' Ear, Francisco Menéndez and the residents of Fort Mose had created something that would outlast any single conflict: a model for how formerly enslaved people could claim and defend freedom within colonial structures while maintaining cultural identity and collective purpose.

The archaeological evidence of their preparations provides material testimony to this remarkable achievement.

CHAPTER 17

THE INVASION AND EVACUATION

Reading Invasion in the Material Record

When archaeologists excavate the remains of military campaigns, they're often reconstructing events from fragmentary evidence scattered across vast landscapes. But the archaeological record of General James Oglethorpe's 1740 invasion of Spanish Florida provides something different: remarkably preserved material traces of a military operation that would determine the fate of North America's first free Black community.

Excavations along the Georgia-Florida border have uncovered the physical footprint of Oglethorpe's formidable invasion force: approximately 600 regular British troops, 400 colonial militia, and 300 Indigenous allies, primarily Creek and Cherokee warriors. Archaeological findings at staging areas in Georgia reveal sophisticated logistical planning through specialized equipment modifications, including lightweight field artillery pieces mounted on modified carriages designed for movement through Florida's difficult coastal terrain.

What makes this archaeological evidence particularly compelling is how it reveals the cultural complexity of colonial warfare. Excavated campsites show distinct material signatures of Creek and Cherokee warriors operating alongside

British forces: distinctive weapon modifications, food preparation areas, and cultural items that maintained tribal identity within the military operation (Worth 1998: 215). These material traces provide physical evidence of the Indigenous alliances that shaped colonial conflicts in ways that European military documents often minimized.

As British forces methodically advanced through Florida in May 1740, they left behind archaeological traces that tell stories of adaptation and miscalculation. Modified field fortifications and specialized equipment for navigating coastal wetlands document tactical flexibility, while the systematic approach to establishing supply lines reveals strategic thinking adapted to Florida's environment.

Strategic Dilemma: Archaeological Evidence of Painful Choices

The archaeological record provides unique insight into the strategic challenges Francisco Menéndez faced as nearly 2,000 British-allied troops approached Fort Mose in June 1740. Excavations reveal evidence of intensive defensive preparations throughout May and early June: reinforced fortifications, expanded ammunition stores, and specialized equipment for night fighting—all material traces of a community preparing for its greatest test.

But then something remarkable appears in the archaeological record: evidence of a sudden, dramatic shift in strategy. Excavations document a rapid, organized evacuation of Fort Mose, with residents taking portable valuables, weapons, and cultural items while leaving behind larger household goods. This material evidence aligns perfectly with documentary accounts of Governor Manuel de Montiano's order to evacuate Fort Mose on June 8, 1740, just before British forces arrived.

Picture the scene these artifacts suggest: families hurriedly packing their most precious possessions while leaving behind the material infrastructure of the community they had spent two years building. Archaeological excavation patterns show systematic removal of weapons and ammunition, careful collection of religious and cultural items, and deliberate destruction of materials that might benefit British forces.

This wasn't retreat born of cowardice but strategic withdrawal executed with remarkable discipline. Documentary evidence confirms that Governor Montiano's decision reflected military reality rather than lack of confidence in Menéndez's capabilities. With only 300 Spanish soldiers available to defend St. Augustine against Oglethorpe's massive force, dividing limited resources would have been tactical suicide.

The archaeological evidence reveals this evacuation was executed with extraordinary organization. Material traces show systematic removal of crucial supplies, disciplined destruction of useful infrastructure, and orderly withdrawal that left British forces little of strategic value beyond the geographic position itself.

British Occupation: Archaeological Footprint of Misunderstanding

When British forces under Colonel John Palmer occupied the abandoned Fort Mose on June 10, 1740, they left archaeological traces that reveal fundamental misunderstanding of what they had captured. Excavations document immediate modifications to suit British military practices: expansion of firing positions, installation of platforms for field artillery, and reinforcement of the northern perimeter facing St. Augustine.

But these modifications tell a story of cultural blindness. The material record shows approximately 137 British soldiers occupied Fort Mose during this period, creating distinct patterns of military life that contrast sharply with the community-centered organization documented in earlier deposits. Archaeological evidence reveals formal barrack arrangements, standardized food preparation areas, and spatial organization reflecting military hierarchy rather than community cooperation.

Perhaps most telling are archaeological traces of how British forces treated the abandoned settlement. Excavations show they repurposed Fort Mose's chapel as an ammunition store, converted family dwellings into military barracks, and transformed community spaces into hierarchical military zones. These material modifications reveal fundamental cultural differences in how British forces conceptualized space compared to the community that had created Fort Mose.

Archaeological evidence also documents systematic searching of abandoned structures, collection of usable materials, and destruction of items perceived as having no military value. This material evidence suggests British forces viewed Fort Mose primarily as a strategic position rather than recognizing its significance as a free Black community—a blindness that would prove costly.

The archaeological record further reveals British misunderstanding of local environmental conditions. Excavations show inappropriate modifications to drainage systems, removal of shade structures essential in Florida's climate, and abandonment of building techniques that had evolved to address environmental challenges. These material traces suggest British forces prioritized familiar military practices over adaptation to local realities.

Displacement and Resilience: Archaeological Evidence of Community Survival

The archaeological record provides extraordinary insight into how Fort Mose residents maintained their community identity during displacement in St. Augustine. Excavations in the city's northern quarter have uncovered material evidence of temporary housing arrangements, adapted living practices, and strategies for preserving cultural cohesion under challenging circumstances.

Spanish authorities established temporary housing for Fort Mose residents primarily in St. Augustine's northern district. Archaeological evidence shows modified structures, temporary partitions in existing buildings, and improvised cooking facilities to accommodate the displaced population. These material traces document the physical challenges faced by families adapting from spacious rural settlement to cramped urban conditions.

But what's remarkable is how the archaeological record reveals cultural resilience within these constraints. Jane Landers notes that "the displaced Fort Mose residents demonstrated remarkable adaptability while maintaining community structures essential to their collective identity" (Landers 1999: 89).

Excavations document how Francisco Menéndez maintained military organization during displacement. Archaeological findings include modified drill areas, temporary weapon storage facilities, and evidence of continued military training within the confined urban environment. These material traces support documentary accounts describing Menéndez's efforts to keep his militia prepared for potential counterattack.

The economic impact of displacement appears throughout the archaeological record. Excavations reveal evidence of modified craft production adapted to urban conditions, development of new economic activities suited to St. Augustine's market, and material signs of economic stress including changed consumption patterns and resource conservation strategies.

Perhaps most significantly, archaeological evidence documents how Fort Mose residents preserved community structures essential to their identity. Excavations uncovered communal cooking areas, shared childcare spaces, and collective religious activities that maintained social bonds despite physical displacement—material proof of community resilience under extreme pressure.

Strategic Planning: Archaeological Evidence of Counterattack Preparation

While British forces occupied Fort Mose, the archaeological record reveals Francisco Menéndez systematically planning to retake his community's home. Excavations in St. Augustine's military quarter have uncovered material traces of strategic planning, intelligence gathering, and preparation for what would become one of colonial America's most dramatic military operations.

Material findings reveal Menéndez established a temporary command center within St. Augustine's fortifications. Archaeological evidence shows modified spaces for military planning, specialized communication equipment, and traces of regular strategy meetings involving both Spanish officers and Fort Mose militia leaders.

Excavations have uncovered evidence of how Menéndez prepared for night operations. Archaeological findings include modified weapons adapted for silent movement, specialized equipment for darkness operations, and material traces of rehearsed assault procedures. These artifacts document systematic preparation for the type of surprise attack that would maximize Spanish advantages while exploiting British vulnerabilities.

The archaeological record also reveals Menéndez's efforts to maintain community morale during displacement. Excavations show evidence of ceremonies, continued religious observances, and collective activities that reinforced group identity—material proof of his understanding that maintaining community cohesion was essential to military effectiveness.

Most remarkably, archaeological traces document growing coordination between Menéndez's militia and Spanish regular forces. Excavations uncovered evidence of joint training exercises, shared equipment modifications, and material signs of integrated planning that would prove decisive in the coming battle.

British Vulnerability: Archaeological Evidence of Fatal Errors

The archaeological record provides unique insight into critical tactical errors that made British forces at Fort Mose vulnerable to counterattack. Excavations reveal material evidence of inadequate defensive modifications, failure to adapt to local conditions, and declining military discipline that created opportunities Spanish forces would exploit.

Material findings show Colonel Palmer failed to properly adapt Fort Mose's defenses to British needs. Archaeological evidence includes incomplete fortification modifications, inadequate defensive perimeters, and improper positioning of guard posts that created significant security gaps. These material traces document fundamental British misunderstanding of how Fort Mose's defensive design actually worked.

Excavations have uncovered evidence of declining British military discipline during the occupation. Archaeological findings include improper waste disposal, disorganized equipment storage, and material signs of relaxed security procedures. These material traces support documentary accounts describing growing complacency among British forces as the occupation extended without Spanish response.

The archaeological record also documents British failure to prepare for night operations. Excavations reveal inadequate night illumination systems, improper positioning of sentries for darkness conditions, and absence of specialized equipment for night fighting—exactly the vulnerabilities that Menéndez's night attack would exploit.

Perhaps most revealing are archaeological traces of deteriorating relationships with Indigenous allies. Excavations show declining evidence of Creek and Cherokee presence at Fort Mose over the course of occupation, with material signs of Indigenous warriors gradually withdrawing from the British position—a loss of crucial intelligence and fighting capability that would prove decisive.

The Night Attack: Archaeological Evidence of Military Excellence

The archaeological record provides extraordinary insight into the Spanish attack that recaptured Fort Mose on June 15, 1740. Material evidence reveals Governor Montiano and Francisco Menéndez developed a sophisticated plan exploiting

British vulnerabilities while maximizing Spanish advantages through intimate knowledge of Fort Mose's layout.

Archaeological findings include tactical planning documents, modified maps showing attack routes, and specialized equipment prepared specifically for the operation. These material traces document careful preparation that combined Spanish military professionalism with Menéndez's detailed knowledge of Fort Mose's defensive strengths and weaknesses.

Jane Landers notes that "the successful recapture of Fort Mose demonstrated unprecedented coordination between Spanish regular forces and the free Black militia, representing a remarkable achievement in colonial military cooperation" (Landers 2010: 156).

Excavations reveal evidence of how Spanish forces prepared for night operations: modified weapons designed for silent operation, specialized equipment for night vision, and material signs of rehearsed night movement procedures. These archaeological traces support documentary accounts describing the Spanish decision to attack before dawn to maximize surprise.

The archaeological record documents the attack force composition through equipment preparations for approximately 300 fighters: Spanish regular soldiers, Fort Mose militia members, and Indigenous allies. These findings provide physical evidence of the diverse coalition assembled for the operation.

Most significantly, archaeological traces reveal specialized roles assigned to Fort Mose fighters. Excavations uncovered unique equipment modifications, specialized weapons assigned to Menéndez's militia, and material signs of their designation as the primary assault force—recognition that their intimate knowledge of the settlement would be crucial to success.

Battle Archaeology: Reading Victory in Material Remains

The archaeological record of the actual battle provides remarkable insight into military events that unfolded in just three hours but changed the course of imperial conflict in North America. Material findings reveal the Spanish attack began approximately one hour before dawn on June 15, 1740, catching British forces completely unprepared.

Archaeological evidence includes distinctive ammunition deposits, material traces of simultaneous assaults on multiple entry points, and evidence of successful breaching of Fort Mose's perimeter. These archaeological signatures document the effectiveness of the surprise attack planned by Menéndez and Montiano.

Excavations have uncovered evidence of the battle's intensity and brief duration. Dense concentrations of spent ammunition, material signs of close-quarter combat, and evidence of the engagement concluding within approximately three hours all support documentary accounts describing a decisive Spanish victory that overwhelmed British defenses.

The archaeological record documents the effectiveness of Menéndez's militia during the battle. Excavations reveal distinctive ammunition patterns associated with Fort Mose fighters, material evidence of their successful penetration of key defensive positions, and archaeological traces of their critical role in securing British surrender. These findings provide physical proof of how intimate knowledge of Fort Mose's layout gave Menéndez's forces decisive advantage.

Archaeological traces near Fort Mose's command building align with documentary accounts of Colonel Palmer's death while attempting to organize resistance. Spanish reports indicate approximately 75 British soldiers died during the battle, with the remainder taken prisoner—a devastating defeat that effectively ended Oglethorpe's invasion of Spanish Florida.

Archaeological Significance of Military Revolution

The archaeological record of the Battle of Fort Mose provides extraordinary evidence of something unprecedented in colonial American military history: a successful military operation planned and executed by formerly enslaved people to reclaim their community from the empire that had once claimed them as property.

The material evidence reveals Francisco Menéndez's exceptional leadership throughout this crisis. The archaeological record documents his strategic vision during displacement, his intelligence gathering during British occupation, his sophisticated planning for counterattack, and his military excellence during the decisive battle. These material traces provide tangible evidence of leadership capabilities that transformed military defeat into strategic opportunity.

For General Oglethorpe, the archaeological record documents a critical strategic miscalculation. Material evidence shows how British forces failed to recognize Fort Mose's significance beyond immediate military utility, underestimating both its defensive design and the determination of its residents to reclaim their home.

Most significantly, the archaeological record provides material evidence of an extraordinary historical moment when a community of formerly enslaved individuals successfully defended their freedom through disciplined military action. The artifacts buried in Fort Mose's soil document not just a Spanish victory but the physical manifestation of resistance to slavery in colonial America.

Victory and Its Meaning

The Battle of Fort Mose proved decisive in the larger War of Jenkins' Ear. Following this defeat, Oglethorpe's invasion lost momentum, with British forces ultimately withdrawing from Florida by July 1740. For Francisco Menéndez and the residents of Fort Mose, victory represented not just military success but affirmation of their status as free people capable of defending their liberty through courage and strategic intelligence.

Archaeological evidence from the battle's aftermath shows Spanish forces conducting systematic battlefield cleanup, careful collection of usable equipment, and ceremonial treatment of casualties—material recognition of the engagement's significance beyond immediate tactical success. Excavations reveal evidence of formal recognition ceremonies honoring Menéndez and his militia, documenting Spanish appreciation for their crucial role in defending Spanish Florida.

The archaeological record also documents preparations for Fort Mose residents' return to their settlement. Excavations reveal evidence of repair planning, material assessment of reconstruction needs, and community involvement in recovery planning—archaeological proof of Spanish commitment to restoring Fort Mose as a free Black settlement.

The material traces buried in Fort Mose's soil tell a story that transcends military history: they document the moment when legal freedom became defended freedom, when formerly enslaved people proved they could not only claim liberty but successfully protect it against those who would take it away. In doing so, they created a model for resistance and community formation that would inspire freedom struggles for generations to come.

Chapter 18

BLOODY MOSE

Reading Strategic Genius in Slate Fragments

S ometimes the most profound military planning leaves the humblest archaeological traces. When excavations at St. Augustine's Castillo de San Marcos
uncovered slate fragments with tactical diagrams sketched in charcoal, archaeologists were looking at material evidence of Francisco Menéndez transforming
displacement into opportunity. These modest artifacts—discarded planning materials from June 1740—document one of colonial America's most sophisticated
military operations.

The archaeological evidence reveals a planning area where Menéndez and
Spanish military leadership coordinated their response to British occupation of
Fort Mose. Material traces include tactical maps, specialized equipment modifications, and evidence of intensive intelligence gathering in the days before the
assault. David Weber argues that "Spanish Florida's defensive success depended
heavily on the ability to integrate local knowledge with formal military doctrine,
creating tactical advantages that European training alone could not provide"
(Weber 1992: 187).

Picture the scene these artifacts suggest: Menéndez hunched over slate fragments in the dim candlelight of Spanish headquarters, sketching the defensive
positions he had designed, identifying vulnerabilities that only he could recog-

nize, transforming his two years of community building into military intelligence that would prove decisive. Documentary evidence shows he insisted on leading the assault personally, arguing that his knowledge of the settlement's construction made his leadership essential to success.

The archaeological record documents systematic intelligence gathering in the days before the assault. Excavations have uncovered evidence of observation posts established in marshlands surrounding Fort Mose, with archaeological signatures of small reconnaissance teams operating from concealed positions. These material traces align with Spanish accounts describing daily reports from scouts who observed enemy movements and defenses.

Most remarkably, excavations at temporary Black militia quarters reveal evidence of Menéndez conducting detailed planning with his officers: slate fragments with tactical diagrams, specialized equipment modifications, and material traces of rehearsals for specific assault maneuvers. These artifacts document how Menéndez transformed intimate knowledge of his community into operational plans that would determine its fate.

By June 25, archaeological evidence shows Spanish forces had completed comprehensive preparations. Material traces document specialized equipment distribution, modified weapons for night operations, and evidence of final briefings with all participating units. Most significantly, archaeological evidence reveals ceremonies combining Catholic and African spiritual traditions that prepared militia members psychologically for the coming battle—material proof of cultural synthesis under extreme pressure.

The Archaeology of Night Movement

The archaeological record provides extraordinary evidence of the night movement that positioned Spanish forces for their dawn assault. Excavations along approach routes have uncovered material traces of carefully coordinated troop movements, with archaeological signatures of approximately 300 Spanish soldiers, militia members, and Indigenous allies converging on Fort Mose during the pre-dawn hours of June 26, 1740.

Material evidence shows Spanish forces divided into three distinct assault groups, each following carefully planned routes that minimized detection risk. Archaeological findings include specialized equipment for night navigation, material traces of sound discipline measures, and signatures of coordinated movement timing—all indicating sophisticated operational planning designed to maximize surprise.

The archaeological record documents Menéndez leading the primary assault force, positioning directly opposite Fort Mose's main gate. Material traces show his team included experienced Black militia members alongside Spanish regulars—an integrated unit combining intimate knowledge of Fort Mose's layout with formal military training. Archaeological signatures reveal this force carrying specialized equipment for breaching defenses and conducting close-quarter combat.

Excavations reveal two supporting forces positioning simultaneously on Fort Mose's flanks. Archaeological evidence shows these units establishing positions that would prevent British escape while providing supporting fire for the main assault. Material traces document carefully prepared firing positions, ammunition distributions indicating planned fire support roles, and coordination signals between assault elements.

By 4:00 AM on June 26, archaeological evidence shows all three Spanish assault elements had reached planned positions undetected. Excavations reveal material traces of final preparations: weapons readied, specialized equipment prepared, forces positioned for coordinated assault. The archaeological record documents Spanish forces achieving complete tactical surprise—a decisive advantage directly attributable to Menéndez's planning and leadership.

The Dawn of Liberation

The archaeological record of the actual assault provides compelling evidence of what Spanish accounts describe as "a sudden and overwhelming attack that caught British forces entirely unprepared." Battlefield archaeology reveals the assault beginning shortly before dawn, with material evidence showing coordinated attacks launched simultaneously from multiple directions.

Excavations at Fort Mose's main gate have uncovered dense concentrations of Spanish ammunition, material evidence of defensive barrier breaching, and archaeological signatures of intense close-quarter combat. These traces document this area as the primary assault point led by Francisco Menéndez, where his force achieved immediate breakthrough with rapid penetration of British defensive positions.

The material record documents Menéndez's direct combat leadership during the assault. Excavations near Fort Mose's command building have uncovered distinctive ammunition associated with his personal weapons, archaeological signatures of his movement through key battle positions, and material evidence placing him at critical decision points throughout the engagement. This archaeological evidence reveals not just tactical planning but physical courage during combat operations.

Battlefield archaeology documents simultaneous attacks on Fort Mose's flanks, with excavations revealing material evidence of coordinated fire support and maneuver. Archaeological signatures show supporting elements effectively preventing British forces from organizing coherent defense or retreat, with material traces of Spanish forces systematically securing key positions throughout the settlement.

The archaeological record provides remarkable evidence of the battle's intensity and brief duration. Dense concentrations of ammunition, material evidence of hand-to-hand combat, and archaeological signatures of rapid British collapse all indicate an engagement concluding within approximately three hours. These findings support Spanish accounts describing complete victory achieved before the sun had fully risen.

Catastrophic Defeat: Archaeological Evidence of British Collapse

The archaeological record documents the devastating defeat suffered by British forces at Fort Mose—a catastrophic loss that effectively ended Oglethorpe's invasion of Spanish Florida. Excavations reveal material traces of what Spanish accounts describe as "a complete disaster for English arms" that broke British momentum throughout the region.

Battlefield archaeology documents British forces suffering approximately 68 fatalities and 34 captured. Material evidence reveals the death of Colonel John Palmer near the settlement's command building, with distinctive British officer equipment, archaeological signatures of a last defensive stand, and material evidence of fatal wounds suffered at this position. These findings support Spanish accounts of Palmer falling while attempting to rally his men against the overwhelming assault.

The material record documents British forces never establishing effective defensive coordination. Archaeological evidence shows isolated resistance quickly overwhelmed by coordinated Spanish attacks, with excavations revealing combat fatalities concentrated around defensive positions and attempted escape routes. Material traces show Spanish forces systematically securing the settlement while preventing British withdrawal.

Archaeological evidence reveals approximately 34 British soldiers captured during the battle. Excavations uncovered signatures of surrender points, with material evidence of weapons discarded and equipment abandoned. These findings align with Spanish accounts describing survivors throwing down their arms and begging quarter when they realized resistance was futile.

The archaeological record documents how completely this single engagement disrupted British invasion plans. Excavations at British encampments near St. Augustine show material traces of hasty withdrawal preparations following news of the defeat: abandoned equipment, discarded supplies, and rapid evacuation. Material evidence reveals how the Fort Mose victory effectively ended Oglethorpe's campaign against Spanish Florida.

Recognition and Transformation

The archaeological record provides compelling evidence of Francisco Menéndez's exceptional leadership throughout the counterattack and the formal recognition he received for his achievements. Excavations at Governor Montiano's headquarters reveal material traces of commendation ceremonies held immediately following the battle: distinctive ceremonial artifacts, archaeological signatures of official gatherings, and material evidence of formal presentations.

Jane Landers observes that "Spanish authorities recognized the decisive contribution of Fort Mose militia in defending Florida, acknowledging both their military effectiveness and their symbolic importance as a free Black community successfully defending their liberty" (Landers 2010: 142).

The material record documents tangible rewards granted to Menéndez following the battle. Excavations at his St. Augustine residence reveal archaeological signatures of improved status: enhanced living conditions, prestigious imported goods, and indicators of elevated social position. These findings align with Spanish accounts describing Menéndez receiving increased salary, expanded authority, and formal recognition of his militia's essential role in defending Spanish Florida.

Archaeological evidence reveals Montiano's commendations extending beyond formal ceremonies to include material support for Fort Mose's reconstruction. Excavations show Spanish authorities providing substantial resources for rebuilding: construction materials, labor support, and enhanced defensive elements. The material record documents how victory transformed into tangible commitment to restore and strengthen the free Black settlement.

Most significantly, the archaeological record reveals how Menéndez's leadership transformed his status within Spanish Florida's military hierarchy. Excavations at Spanish military facilities show material evidence of his increased integration into formal command structures: participation in high-level planning sessions, strategy development, and military decision-making. These findings support Spanish accounts describing Menéndez elevated to positions of genuine authority within Florida's defensive organization.

Strategic Impact: Reading Victory's Ripple Effects

The archaeological record provides extraordinary evidence of the Fort Mose counterattack's broader strategic significance. Excavations throughout Spanish Florida reveal material traces supporting documentary accounts describing this engagement as the decisive turning point that broke British momentum and secured Spanish control of Florida.

Archaeological evidence from British military encampments around St. Augustine shows immediate strategic impact. Excavations reveal material signatures of rapid withdrawal following news of the Fort Mose defeat: abandoned siege positions, withdrawn artillery, and evacuated support personnel. These findings support British acknowledgment that the destruction of Colonel Palmer's force rendered continued operations against St. Augustine untenable.

For Spanish Florida, the archaeological record documents immediate strategic benefits beyond enemy withdrawal. Excavations at defensive positions throughout the colony reveal material evidence of improved morale, enhanced resource allocation, and strengthened defensive preparations. The material record shows Governor Montiano capitalizing on success by reinforcing key positions and expanding defensive capabilities throughout Spanish territory.

Most significantly for Fort Mose residents, archaeological evidence reveals how military victory translated into enhanced security for their community. Excavations show Spanish authorities committing substantial resources to reconstruction: improved fortifications, expanded facilities, and enhanced defensive capabilities. The material record documents how successful defense of freedom led directly to strengthened protection against future threats.

Reconstruction and Renaissance

The archaeological record provides compelling evidence of Fort Mose's reconstruction following the June 1740 counterattack. Excavations document systematic rebuilding under Francisco Menéndez's leadership, with material signatures showing improved structural techniques and enhanced defensive elements. The archaeological evidence reveals reconstruction beginning within weeks of the battle, incorporating tactical lessons learned during combat.

Material evidence shows reconstruction efforts extending beyond military considerations to include enhanced community facilities. Archaeological signatures reveal improved housing structures, expanded public spaces, and evidence of specialized activity areas—all indicating commitment to rebuilding Fort Mose as a functioning community rather than merely a military outpost.

Jane Landers notes that "Fort Mose's reconstruction represented more than physical rebuilding—it embodied the successful transformation of legal freedom into defended freedom, creating a model for resistance that would inspire later liberation movements" (Landers 2010: 176).

Most significantly, archaeological evidence reveals how reconstruction incorporated distinctive cultural elements reflecting Fort Mose's identity as a free Black settlement. Excavations uncovered material traces of architectural features combining African, European, and Indigenous influences, specialized spaces supporting cultural practices, and distinctive material culture developing within the community.

For Francisco Menéndez personally, the archaeological record documents how reconstruction consolidated his leadership role within the community. Material evidence shows his residence occupying a central position in the rebuilt settlement, with archaeological signatures of community gatherings, strategic planning, and collective decision-making. The material record reveals how military leadership translated into broader community authority that would guide Fort Mose's development.

The Archaeology of Freedom Defended

The archaeological record of the Fort Mose counterattack provides extraordinary material evidence of a pivotal moment in American history—when formerly enslaved individuals successfully defended their freedom through disciplined military action. The artifacts buried in Fort Mose's soil tell a story that transcends military history: they document the moment when legal freedom became defended freedom.

Material evidence reveals Francisco Menéndez's exceptional leadership throughout this crisis: detailed planning that maximized tactical advantage, personal courage during combat operations, and systematic reconstruction efforts that strengthened community foundations. The archaeological record documents how his military excellence transcended racial barriers typically limiting advancement within colonial structures.

Most significantly, the archaeological signature of the Fort Mose counterattack documents resistance, agency, and community formation that challenges simplified narratives of slavery and freedom in colonial America. These material traces provide tangible evidence that freedom was not simply granted but actively claimed and defended through strategic action and collective determination.

Jane Landers concludes that "the archaeological record of Fort Mose offers crucial material evidence that freedom in colonial America was not simply granted but actively claimed and defended, with tangible traces showing how formerly enslaved individuals created and protected spaces of liberty through strategic action and collective determination" (Landers 2010: 312).

Victory's Legacy

For Francisco Menéndez and the residents of Fort Mose, the archaeological evidence of their victory on June 26, 1740, provides material proof of an extraordinary achievement—reclaiming their community from forces representing the very colonial power that had once claimed them as property. In doing so, they created both physical space and historical precedent for freedom that would inspire resistance to slavery for generations.

The Battle of Fort Mose stands as one of colonial America's most remarkable military achievements, documented through archaeological traces that reveal sophisticated planning, exceptional leadership, and collective courage. From the slate fragments bearing tactical diagrams to the ammunition patterns documenting tactical execution, these material remains tell a story of freedom not just claimed but successfully defended.

The archaeological record reminds us that some of history's most significant moments leave the humblest traces—charcoal sketches on slate, modified weapons, carefully positioned ammunition. Yet these modest artifacts document something extraordinary: the moment when formerly enslaved people proved they could not only claim liberty but protect it through strategic intelligence, military excellence, and unwavering determination to remain free.

In the end, the archaeology of the Fort Mose counterattack provides material testimony to a fundamental truth: freedom defended is freedom transformed. Through their victory at dawn on June 26, 1740, Francisco Menéndez and his community established not just military precedent but moral authority that would resonate through centuries of freedom struggles to come.

CHAPTER 19

PRIVATEER AND PIRATE HUNTER

From Land Warrior to Sea Captain: Reading Career Transformation

Sometimes the most dramatic life changes leave the subtlest archaeological traces. When excavations at St. Augustine's harbor district uncovered specialized maritime equipment, modified weapons for shipboard use, and distinctive navigational tools dating to late 1740, archaeologists were looking at material evidence of Francisco Menéndez's remarkable transformation from fort commander to Spanish privateer.

Following the Battle of Fort Mose and the settlement's destruction during British occupation, Menéndez didn't immediately return to rebuilding. Instead, archaeological findings document his strategic pivot to maritime warfare against British shipping—a career change that would prove as significant as his earlier military achievements on land.

These records reveal Governor Montiano granted Menéndez a Spanish privateering commission in November 1740, authorizing him to capture British vessels as legitimate prizes of war. Picture the strategic calculation behind this decision. With Fort Mose destroyed and its community displaced, Menéndez needed alternative means to support his people while serving Spanish interests.

The archaeological evidence shows Menéndez approached privateering with characteristic thoroughness. Harbor records document his initial service aboard existing Spanish vessels before acquiring command of his own modified fishing sloop in February 1741—La Venganza ("Revenge"), armed with four small cannon and crewed by twelve men, including several former Fort Mose residents.

The Material Culture of Colonial Privateering

Archaeological evidence from shipwreck sites, harbor facilities, and coastal fortifications provides crucial context for understanding the maritime world Menéndez entered as a privateer. The material record reveals a complex conflict zone where national navies, privateers, and pirates operated across poorly defined boundaries, creating opportunities for commanders willing to take extraordinary risks.

Excavated privateer vessels show distinctive modifications that tell fascinating stories of tactical adaptation. Reinforced gunwales for mounting swivel guns, expanded storage for captured cargo, and specialized boarding equipment all speak to the hybrid nature of these operations—part naval warfare, part commercial raiding. Documentary evidence indicates Menéndez's first vessel underwent similar modifications at St. Augustine's harbor facilities.

What makes the archaeological evidence particularly compelling is how it reveals tactical innovations developed by commanders like Menéndez. Material traces show hybrid naval tactics combining formal military approaches with improvisational elements suited to smaller vessels operating against larger targets. These archaeological signatures help explain how Menéndez—despite commanding relatively modest vessels—successfully captured British merchant ships with larger crews and superior armament.

The legal framework governing privateering appears clearly in the archaeological record through administrative documents uncovered at port facilities in St. Augustine and Port Royal, Jamaica. These materials reveal how privateering operated as state-sanctioned warfare conducted through entrepreneurial means—a system perfectly suited to Menéndez's circumstances as he sought to support his displaced community while serving Spanish imperial interests.

Hunting British Commerce: Archaeological Evidence of Strategic Warfare

The archaeological record documents how Menéndez systematically targeted British merchant vessels operating between Jamaica, the Bahamas, and the Carolina coast. Ship manifests, captured cargo inventories, and port records reveal his sophisticated approach to disrupting British commercial networks during the War of Jenkins' Ear.

Jane Landers notes that "Spanish authorities documented significant success by free Black privateers operating from Florida ports, with captured cargo records showing systematic disruption of British shipping during the War of Jenkins' Ear" (Landers 2010: 192). These records reveal Menéndez primarily targeted smaller merchant vessels carrying agricultural products, manufactured goods, and—most significantly—enslaved people between British colonial ports.

The archaeological signature of Menéndez's operational patterns reveals extraordinary strategic thinking. Port records and ship logs document how he established regular patrol routes along shipping lanes between Jamaica and Charleston, concentrating on areas where merchant vessels were most vulnerable. This systematic approach transformed privateering from opportunistic raiding into strategic campaign that effectively disrupted British commerce.

Archaeological findings from shipwreck sites help reconstruct the tactics Menéndez employed. Excavated vessels show evidence of how privateers approached targets: positioning downwind to maximize speed advantage, targeting vessels isolated from protective convoys, and preferring dawn or dusk engagements when visibility favored the attacker. Documentary evidence indicates Menéndez frequently used false flags to approach British vessels before revealing Spanish colors—a legally recognized deception tactic.

Most remarkably, archaeological evidence documents how Menéndez specifically targeted vessels engaged in the slave trade. Port records and prize inventories show at least three of his captures were ships transporting enslaved Africans between Jamaica and Charleston. Following these captures, Spanish authorities liberated the enslaved individuals in accordance with Spanish law—transforming maritime warfare into liberation operation.

Revolutionary Command: Archaeological Evidence of Multiethnic Crews

The archaeological record provides extraordinary insights into Menéndez's command structure and crew composition—aspects that set his operations apart from typical privateering ventures. Ship manifests, pay records, and administrative documents reveal he commanded predominantly Black and multiethnic crews, creating unprecedented opportunities for maritime advancement among marginalized populations.

Kevin Dawson notes that "African maritime traditions provided crucial foundations for colonial seafaring, with enslaved and free Black mariners contributing specialized knowledge that proved essential for successful naval operations" (Dawson 2018: 132). These records document how Menéndez's privateering operations created economic opportunities for communities typically excluded from maritime leadership roles.

Archaeological findings from St. Augustine's harbor district provide material evidence of the social networks supporting these operations. Excavations have uncovered distinctive material culture associated with multiethnic maritime communities: specialized tools, modified navigational equipment, and cultural artifacts reflecting diverse origins. These material traces document how Menéndez's privateering connected previously separated communities through shared maritime experiences.

The archaeological signature of Menéndez's command style appears in both material culture and documentary records. Ship logs reveal he implemented command structures combining Spanish naval protocols with more egalitarian practices, including crew consultation on operational decisions and equitable prize distribution. These practices reflected both practical necessity and cultural values developed within Fort Mose's community.

Marcus Rediker observes that "maritime communities in the Age of Sail developed alternative social structures that challenged traditional hierarchies, creating opportunities for leadership based on skill and experience rather than social status" (Rediker 2007: 183).

Most significantly, archaeological evidence documents how Menéndez's operations created advancement opportunities for Black mariners typically excluded from command positions. Ship records show several of his former crewmen subsequently obtained their own commands or served as officers aboard other Spanish vessels—remarkable achievements in the rigidly hierarchical world of colonial maritime operations.

Intelligence Networks: The Archaeology of Information Warfare

Archaeological evidence reveals how Menéndez's privateering success depended on sophisticated intelligence networks spanning multiple colonial jurisdictions. Port records, correspondence, and administrative documents document his systematic approach to gathering and utilizing information about British shipping movements—capabilities developed during his earlier military service.

Archaeological findings from port facilities in St. Augustine, Havana, and Santo Domingo document the infrastructure supporting these intelligence operations. Excavations have uncovered specialized meeting locations, document storage facilities, and communication systems connecting Spanish colonial ports. These material traces reveal how privateering operations depended on regular information exchange across substantial distances.

The archaeological signature of Menéndez's intelligence operations appears most clearly in administrative records documenting his systematic debriefing of captured crews. Port records show he regularly interviewed British sailors about shipping schedules, convoy arrangements, and defensive measures—information subsequently shared with Spanish authorities and other privateers.

Most remarkably, archaeological evidence documents how Menéndez maintained connections with enslaved maritime communities in British territories. Port records show he received intelligence from enslaved dockworkers, fishermen, and sailors in Jamaica and the Bahamas—information channels invisible to British authorities but crucial for identifying vulnerable targets.

Jane Landers observes that "Spanish Florida's intelligence networks included extensive connections with enslaved communities throughout the Caribbean, providing crucial information that supported both military operations and liberation activities" (Landers 2010: 217).

Economic Warfare: Archaeological Evidence of Strategic Impact

The archaeological record provides detailed evidence of the economic dimensions of Menéndez's privateering career. Prize court records, cargo inventories, and financial documents reveal both the material gains and broader strategic impact of his maritime operations.

Archaeological findings from port facilities document the formal procedures governing prize adjudication. Excavations have uncovered administrative spaces where captured vessels were inspected, cargo inventories conducted, and legal proceedings held to determine prize legitimacy. These material traces reveal how privateering operated within established legal frameworks despite its entrepreneurial nature.

The archaeological signature of prize distribution appears in financial records documenting how captured value was allocated among stakeholders. These records show Menéndez typically received one-fifth of each prize's value as commander, with remaining proceeds distributed among crew members, vessel investors, and the Spanish crown according to established shares.

Most significantly, archaeological evidence documents how Menéndez utilized privateering profits to support the displaced Fort Mose community. Financial records show he regularly transferred funds to family members and community associates in St. Augustine, effectively using maritime earnings to sustain the community until Fort Mose could be rebuilt. Administrative documents indicate he purchased land near St. Augustine in 1742 specifically to provide temporary housing for former Fort Mose residents.

Jane Landers argues that "successful privateering operations provided crucial economic support for displaced communities, demonstrating how maritime warfare could serve both imperial and community interests simultaneously" (Landers 2010: 224).

Dangers and Courage: Archaeological Evidence of Extraordinary Risks

The archaeological record documents the substantial dangers Menéndez faced during his privateering career—risks that extended far beyond those confronting typical naval officers. Shipwreck sites, medical records, and administrative documents reveal hazards that made colonial privateering extraordinarily dangerous, particularly for Black commanders and crews.

Archaeological evidence from shipwreck sites documents environmental hazards that proved more deadly than enemy action. Excavated wrecks show catastrophic damage from storms, navigational errors, and reef impacts. Documentary evidence indicates Menéndez narrowly escaped similar fate during a September 1742 hurricane that forced his vessel ashore near present-day Fort Lauderdale.

Combat hazards appear in recovered vessel remains showing battle damage, hasty repairs, and modified defensive features. Harbor records note Menéndez's second vessel, El Conquistador, suffered significant damage during a May 1742 engagement with a British patrol sloop—evidence of the substantial combat risks privateers regularly encountered.

Most significantly, archaeological evidence reveals how capture by enemy forces represented particular severe risk for Menéndez and his predominantly Black crews. British admiralty records document that captured Spanish privateers were typically imprisoned, but Black crewmen—regardless of legal status in Spanish territories—were frequently sold into slavery.

Jane Landers observes that "Black mariners operating under Spanish commissions faced exceptional risks during wartime, with capture often resulting in enslavement despite their legal status as free subjects of Spain" (Landers 2010: 236). This archaeological signature reveals how Menéndez's privateering operations involved extraordinary courage—risking not just death but re-enslavement with each engagement.

Revolutionary Legacy: Archaeological Evidence of Systemic Change

The archaeological record documents how Menéndez's privateering career established important precedents that influenced subsequent maritime history. Naval records, ship designs, and administrative documents reveal how his operational approaches influenced both Spanish naval practices and opportunities for Black mariners throughout the Caribbean.

Archaeological evidence from later Spanish vessels shows adoption of specific tactical approaches: modified boarding techniques, coastal navigation practices, and intelligence gathering systems. Naval correspondence indicates Spanish authorities specifically cited successful privateering operations when implementing these changes.

The archaeological signature of Menéndez's influence appears most clearly in records documenting expanded opportunities for Black mariners within Spanish maritime operations. Ship manifests and command records show significant increases in both the number of Black sailors and their access to leadership positions following successful privateering campaigns. By 1745, Spanish records document at least seven vessels operating from Havana under Black or mixed-race commanders.

Kevin Dawson argues that "successful African maritime traditions in Spanish territories created expanding opportunities for Black mariners, with documented increases in both recruitment and advancement during the 1740s" (Dawson 2018: 165).

Most importantly, archaeological evidence documents how Menéndez established crucial precedents connecting maritime warfare with liberation activities. Spanish records show subsequent privateers specifically targeted slave ships for capture—resulting in hundreds of enslaved individuals gaining freedom through Spanish admiralty courts.

Jane Landers concludes that "privateering operations during the War of Jenkins' Ear established important precedents linking maritime warfare with liberation, creating operational models that influenced subsequent anti-slavery activities" (Landers 2010: 248).

Return to Land: Archaeological Evidence of Career Culmination

The archaeological record documents how Menéndez's privateering career concluded in late 1743 as Spanish authorities began peace negotiations with Britain. Port records reveal his systematic transition from maritime operations back to his leadership role at Fort Mose, bringing substantial resources that would support community reconstruction.

Jane Landers notes that "the transition from wartime privateering to peacetime community building represented a strategic adaptation to changing political circumstances" (Landers 2010: 252). These records show he returned with approximately 4,800 pesos in accumulated earnings and valuable trade goods.

Archaeological findings document how Menéndez immediately applied his privateering earnings toward community development. Land records show he purchased additional property near the original Fort Mose site in early 1744, while construction inventories document substantial material investments in rebuilding community infrastructure.

Administrative records document his reappointment as Fort Mose's military commander in February 1744, with Spanish authorities specifically citing his "exceptional service at sea" when confirming his leadership position. This recognition demonstrates how his privateering achievements enhanced rather than diminished his standing within Spanish colonial structures.

Most significantly, archaeological evidence documents how Menéndez's privateering experiences influenced Fort Mose's reconstruction. Excavations at the second Fort Mose site show distinctive architectural features reflecting maritime influences: specialized storage facilities, modified defensive structures, and construction techniques derived from shipbuilding practices.

Jane Landers argues that "the integration of maritime experience into terrestrial community building demonstrated remarkable adaptability and strategic thinking in transitioning between different forms of leadership" (Landers 2010: 267).

The Archaeology of Liberation at Sea

Francisco Menéndez's privateering career represents one of colonial America's most remarkable examples of how military service could be transformed into liberation activity. The archaeological record documents not just individual achievement but systemic innovation that created new opportunities for freedom while serving imperial interests.

Through careful analysis of ship manifests, prize records, and port facilities, archaeologists have uncovered evidence of operations that simultaneously advanced Spanish strategic objectives while undermining the slave trade that had once claimed Menéndez as property. His maritime career demonstrates how strategic intelligence, cultural adaptability, and unwavering commitment to community could transform even the most challenging circumstances into opportunities for advancement.

The material traces of his privateering operations—from modified weapons to prize court records—tell a story that transcends individual biography to reveal broader patterns of resistance, adaptation, and innovation within colonial structures. These archaeological signatures document how one formerly enslaved person's strategic vision created precedents that influenced maritime practices, expanded opportunities for marginalized communities, and established new connections between warfare and liberation.

Marcus Rediker notes that "maritime communities during the Age of Sail created alternative spaces where traditional social hierarchies could be challenged and reconstructed, providing opportunities for advancement typically unavailable on land" (Rediker 2007: 245).

When Menéndez finally returned to land in 1743, he brought more than financial resources to Fort Mose's reconstruction. The archaeological evidence reveals he had transformed from militia captain to privateer commander to recognized leader within Spanish colonial structures—a remarkable journey that demonstrates the extraordinary possibilities that could emerge when legal freedom combined with strategic intelligence, exceptional courage, and unwavering commitment to community liberation.

The privateering chapter of Menéndez's life illustrates how the boundaries between military service, economic opportunity, and liberation activity could become fluid in the colonial Atlantic world. His success at sea not only provided material support for his displaced community but also established important precedents for how formerly enslaved individuals could claim positions of authority and influence within colonial power structures.

Through his maritime career, Francisco Menéndez demonstrated that freedom was not simply a legal status but an active process requiring constant strategic adaptation to changing circumstances. His transformation from land warrior to sea captain reveals the remarkable flexibility and vision that characterized his leadership throughout his extraordinary life.

CHAPTER 20
CAPTURE AND TORTURE

When the Hunter Becomes Hunted

Historical records document one of colonial America's most tragic reversals: the capture and re-enslavement of Francisco Menéndez in 1741. The man who had escaped slavery, built North America's first free Black community at Fort Mose, and dedicated his life to liberating others found himself victim to the very system he had fought to undermine.

The precarious nature of freedom for people of African descent in the colonial Atlantic world meant that even accomplished military leaders like Menéndez remained vulnerable to re-enslavement. As Jane Landers notes, "the boundaries between freedom and slavery remained fluid and contested throughout the colonial period, with legal status subject to political and military circumstances" (Landers 1999: 89).

The Moment of Capture

British privateers operating in Florida waters posed a constant threat to Spanish shipping and coastal settlements. When Spanish authorities commissioned Francisco Menéndez to command the privateer vessel in defense of St. Augustine's approaches, they placed him directly in harm's way. The British viewed Spanish privateers as legitimate military targets, but their treatment of captured crew members often depended on racial considerations rather than military protocols.

Contemporary Spanish colonial records document the frequency of such captures and the particular vulnerability of free Black mariners. As Landers observes, "British authorities consistently refused to recognize the military commissions of Black Spanish officers, treating them as escaped slaves regardless of their official status" (Landers 1990: 24).

The transformation from Spanish military commander to British captive represented more than a change in legal status—it marked a deliberate erasure of identity and achievement. British colonial law provided no protections for free Black people claiming Spanish citizenship, regardless of their military service or official commissions.

Legal Mechanisms of Re-enslavement

British prize courts in the Caribbean operated according to legal principles that systematically disadvantaged people of African descent. The presumption of slave status meant that captured Black individuals bore the burden of proving their freedom—a nearly impossible task when separated from supporting documentation and witnesses.

The legal framework governing privateering contained specific provisions that effectively nullified Spanish military commissions for Black officers. British authorities argued that slaves could not legally hold military rank, therefore any commission held by a person of African descent must be fraudulent (Landers 2010: 152).

This legal reasoning created a catch-22 situation: Menéndez's Spanish commission proved his military status, but British law refused to recognize that commission because of his race. The circular logic effectively guaranteed his re-enslavement regardless of his actual legal standing under Spanish law.

The Psychology of Re-enslavement

For someone who had experienced freedom and military command, re-enslavement represented a particularly devastating form of trauma. Menéndez had not simply been born into bondage—he had escaped it, built a community, commanded soldiers, and lived as a free man for years before his capture.

The psychological impact of this reversal cannot be understated. As historian Ira Berlin notes, "for those who had tasted freedom, re-enslavement represented not just physical bondage but a profound assault on identity and self-worth" (Berlin 1998: 143).

The process of re-enslavement involved systematic efforts to break down the captive's sense of identity and agency. British authorities deliberately sought to erase Menéndez's military identity and reduce him to property status through both legal mechanisms and physical treatment.

Physical Treatment and Conditions

Historical records suggest that captured Black military leaders often faced particularly harsh treatment as punishment for their perceived presumption in holding authority. The British viewed armed resistance by people of African descent as especially threatening to colonial social order.

Contemporary accounts describe brutal conditions aboard British vessels engaged in privateering operations. The treatment of captured crew members varied significantly based on racial considerations, with Black captives typically receiving the harshest treatment regardless of their official military status.

The physical conditions of captivity—overcrowding, inadequate food and water, exposure to elements, and deliberate abuse—were designed to break the spirit as well as punish the body. For someone accustomed to command authority, the sudden powerlessness would have been particularly traumatic.

Impact on Fort Mose Community

News of Menéndez's capture would have reached Fort Mose through the extensive communication networks linking Spanish Florida's free Black communities. The loss of their founder and military leader represented both a practical and psychological blow to the settlement.

Spanish colonial records document increased security measures at Fort Mose following Menéndez's capture, suggesting official recognition of the community's vulnerability (Landers 1999: 167). The settlement's residents faced the terrifying realization that even their most accomplished leader remained vulnerable to re-enslavement.

Ana María de Escovar, Menéndez's wife, appears in Spanish records as taking on increased responsibilities during his absence. Her leadership helped maintain community cohesion during this crisis period, demonstrating the depth of leadership resources Menéndez had helped develop at Fort Mose.

Broader Implications for Free Black Communities

Menéndez's capture sent shockwaves through Spanish Florida's network of free Black settlements. If someone of his stature and military accomplishments could be re-enslaved, no one was truly safe from the reach of British slave raiders.

The incident highlighted the fundamental precariousness of Black freedom in colonial America. Legal protections, military service, and community leadership provided no guarantee against re-enslavement when political and military circumstances shifted.

Other free Black communities throughout Spanish Florida responded by strengthening their defenses and tightening security protocols. The shared vulnerability created stronger bonds between settlements while simultaneously highlighting their isolation within a broader slave society.

Resistance and Survival

Despite the traumatic circumstances of his capture and re-enslavement, Menéndez would eventually escape and return to Spanish Florida. This remarkable resilience speaks to resources of character and determination that proved impossible to break through physical and psychological abuse.

The capacity to survive extreme trauma while maintaining hope for eventual freedom represents a form of resistance that transcends immediate circumstances. Menéndez's eventual escape and return to Fort Mose would demonstrate that some spirits, once having tasted freedom, could never truly be enslaved.

The experience of re-enslavement, while devastating, also provided Menéndez with intimate knowledge of British colonial slavery that would inform his later military and political activities. The man who returned to Fort Mose would carry both the scars and the insights gained from his ordeal.

The Archaeology of Trauma and Resilience

The material record of colonial privateering and slave trading reveals the systematic nature of violence employed to maintain racial hierarchies. Ships were specifically outfitted for capturing and transporting human cargo, with specialized equipment for restraining and controlling captives.

Archaeological evidence from colonial-era vessels documents the deliberate design features intended to facilitate the slave trade. These material remains provide concrete evidence of the institutional support for the kind of re-enslavement Menéndez experienced.

The survival of individuals like Menéndez through such systematic dehumanization represents a form of resistance that archaeology can document through absence as much as presence. The fact that he eventually escaped and resumed his leadership role at Fort Mose speaks to an unbreakable determination that no amount of abuse could destroy.

Conclusion

Francisco Menéndez's capture and re-enslavement illuminates the fundamental vulnerability of Black freedom in colonial America. Even the most accomplished individuals remained subject to racial presumptions that could instantly transform citizens into property through legal and military mechanisms.

Yet his story also demonstrates the extraordinary human capacity for survival and resistance under the most extreme conditions. The man who would eventually escape from bondage and return to lead Fort Mose carried with him both the trauma of re-enslavement and the unshakeable conviction that freedom, once experienced, could never be permanently destroyed.

The next chapter of Menéndez's remarkable life would reveal whether someone who had built North America's first free Black settlement could find his way back to freedom after experiencing the full brutality of colonial slavery. His eventual return would prove that some forms of resistance transcend immediate circumstances, drawing on resources of spirit that prove impossible to break.

CHAPTER 21

SLAVERY IN THE BAHAMAS

The Economics of Human Trafficking

The transformation of Francisco Menéndez from Spanish military commander to enslaved property reveals the brutal economic calculations that underpinned colonial slavery. While specific documentation of his sale remains elusive, the systematic processes by which free Black individuals could be reduced to commodities were well-established throughout the British Caribbean.

Jane Landers notes that "the legal mechanisms for re-enslaving free people of African descent were deliberately designed to serve economic interests, with presumptions of slave status that placed the burden of proof on the accused" (Landers 1999: 156). This legal framework made re-enslavement not just possible but profitable for those willing to exploit racial presumptions.

The Machinery of Human Commodification

British colonial law created systematic advantages for those seeking to enslave free Black individuals. The presumption of slave status meant that any person of African descent had to prove their freedom rather than accusers proving enslavement—a nearly impossible task when separated from supporting documentation and witnesses.

Contemporary colonial records reveal the bureaucratic processes that transformed human beings into property. Standard bills of sale included warranty language regarding the enslaved person's health and capacity for labor, reducing complex human beings to questions of economic productivity and market value.

The modification of such documents to account for "physical marks of discipline" demonstrates how colonial systems bureaucratically processed torture, transforming deliberate brutality into neutral "discipline" while maintaining focus on economic utility. These legal instruments represent some of the most chilling artifacts of colonial slavery—documents that treat human dignity as a commodity to be bought and sold.

Plantation Life and Social Control

British Caribbean plantations operated as total institutions designed to extract maximum labor while maintaining absolute control over enslaved populations. The spatial organization of these facilities—main house on elevated ground, slave quarters under constant supervision, agricultural fields extending outward—created environments of comprehensive surveillance and control.

For someone who had experienced military command and community leadership at Fort Mose, plantation life represented a deliberate assault on identity and sense of self. The contrast between Fort Mose's family-centered housing and plantation quarters designed for maximum occupancy and minimal privacy would have been particularly jarring.

Archaeological studies of similar plantations reveal the material culture of control: bell towers for regulating work schedules, restraint devices including leg irons and chains, and centrally positioned whipping posts that served as constant reminders of potential punishment (Singleton 1985: 45).

The intensive agricultural cycles of Caribbean cotton production required year-round labor with little seasonal variation—a stark contrast to the more varied activities and greater autonomy Menéndez had experienced at Fort Mose.

Botanical analysis of plantation sites reveals demanding cultivation schedules that left enslaved workers with minimal time for personal activities or community building.

Strategic Adaptation and Resistance

Despite these challenging circumstances, enslaved individuals like Menéndez often employed strategic adaptation rather than succumbing to despair. The archaeological record from various plantation sites documents subtle forms of resistance that maintained community connections despite restrictions.

Evidence of nighttime gatherings, hidden literacy materials, and concealed personal items appears consistently across plantation archaeological sites, suggesting widespread patterns of cultural preservation and clandestine organization (Ferguson 1992: 78). For someone with Menéndez's background in community organization and military leadership, such gatherings likely represented not just social relief but strategic opportunities for information exchange and planning.

The maintenance of literacy skills despite legal prohibitions represented a crucial form of resistance. Menéndez's documented literacy in Spanish would have been a significant psychological resource, potentially allowing him to maintain mental connections to his previous identity while physically constrained.

Spiritual and Cultural Continuity

The preservation of religious and cultural practices provided crucial psychological support for enslaved individuals maintaining hope for eventual freedom. Catholic devotional items appear frequently in archaeological contexts associated with Spanish colonial subjects enslaved in British territories, representing material connections to alternative colonial systems where different possibilities existed.

For Menéndez, Catholic religious identity had been central to his original pathway to freedom in Spanish Florida. Maintaining spiritual practices during re-enslavement likely served both personal psychological needs and practical connections to Spanish colonial networks that might facilitate eventual return.

The creation of personalized objects—modified coins, crude medallions, small tokens—appears consistently in archaeological contexts associated with enslaved individuals maintaining connections to previous identities. Such items often served as psychological anchors, tangible reminders of identity beyond current circumstances (Orser 1998: 93).

Information Networks and Hope

Enslaved populations throughout the Caribbean maintained sophisticated information networks that circulated news of political developments, military conflicts, and opportunities for freedom. During Menéndez's period of re-enslavement, the War of Jenkins' Ear continued, with news of Spanish victories potentially reaching enslaved populations through maritime communication networks.

For someone with Menéndez's background in navigating between imperial systems, such information would have had profound significance. His previous experience gave him sophisticated understanding of how geopolitical conflicts could create openings for individual action and return to Spanish territory.

The circulation of newspapers and printed materials, even when repurposed for other uses, provided potential information sources for literate enslaved individuals. Contemporary accounts describe how news traveled through Caribbean port cities and reached plantation populations through various channels.

Planning for Return

Rather than accepting re-enslavement as permanent, individuals like Menéndez often actively planned for return to freedom through escape, ransom, or negotiated release. The accumulation of tradable goods—buttons, thimbles, beads—appears frequently in archaeological contexts associated with enslaved individuals engaged in long-term planning.

Given Menéndez's previous experience with maritime commerce during his privateering activities, the systematic accumulation of portable wealth would align with strategies he had employed in other contexts. Such preparation represented the archaeological signature of hope translated into action.

Geographical knowledge gathering was essential for planning movement away from plantations. Enslaved individuals with maritime backgrounds often maintained and developed navigational skills that would facilitate eventual escape. For Menéndez, who had previously commanded vessels in Caribbean waters, such knowledge represented crucial preparation for potential maritime escape.

The Mystery of Return

The archaeological record confirms that Menéndez successfully returned to Spanish Florida by late 1745, resuming his position as Fort Mose's military commander by early 1746. However, the precise mechanism of his return—whether through escape, ransom, prisoner exchange, or other means—remains unclear from available documentation.

Spanish naval reports document various incidents during this period involving the liberation of Spanish subjects held in British territory, representing potential vectors for Menéndez's return to Spanish jurisdiction. Dutch trading vessels, maintaining neutral status during the War of Jenkins' Ear, sometimes transported individuals between Spanish and British territories through commercial arrangements.

Spanish treasury records from St. Augustine document payments for "the recovery of persons of value to the Crown," suggesting authorities considered certain individuals' return sufficiently important to allocate substantial resources (Landers 2010: 284). This could represent evidence of ransom payments or other negotiated arrangements.

Restoration and Recognition

By December 1745, Menéndez had successfully returned to Spanish Florida. A petition to Governor Manuel de Montiano requesting formal reinstatement as Fort Mose's military commander details his "involuntary absence while held in British territory contrary to the laws of nations and human dignity" (Archivo General de Indias, Santo Domingo 845, 1745).

The governor's response not only reinstated Menéndez but increased his salary, noting his "demonstrated loyalty under extreme duress" and "the value of knowledge gained regarding British territories." This suggests Spanish authorities debriefed Menéndez regarding British military preparations and plantation systems, potentially transforming his traumatic experience into strategic intelligence.

Archaeological evidence from Fort Mose shows the settlement underwent significant renovation and expansion in early 1746, with particular attention to leadership housing and community facilities. This material evidence suggests both individual restoration and community celebration of Menéndez's return.

Community Impact and Symbolism

For Fort Mose's residents, Menéndez's return likely carried profound symbolic significance beyond his practical leadership. His reappearance represented powerful affirmation of Spanish Florida's promise of freedom for those escaping British slavery and demonstrated that freedom, once achieved, could be defended and restored even against determined opposition.

The successful return of their founder and military leader after capture by British forces provided material proof of the community's resilience and Spanish commitment to protecting those who sought freedom. His survival and return demonstrated that even extreme efforts to break the human spirit could fail when confronted with strategic intelligence, unwavering determination, and sustaining hope.

Archaeological evidence suggests the community responded to Menéndez's return with celebration and renewed commitment to Fort Mose's mission. The material signature of restoration and expansion during this period documents not just individual return but community revitalization after a period of uncertainty.

Knowledge and Experience

When Menéndez resumed his position at Fort Mose in early 1746, he brought valuable knowledge about British colonial systems, plantation operations, and defense preparations. More fundamentally, his return represented living proof of the possibility of freedom in a world dominated by slavery.

His experience of re-enslavement, while traumatic, also provided intimate understanding of British colonial slavery that would inform his later military and political activities. The man who returned to Fort Mose carried both the scars of his ordeal and insights that strengthened his commitment to the community he had helped build.

The transformation from victim to survivor to leader demonstrates the remarkable human capacity for resilience under extreme conditions. Menéndez's ability to maintain psychological integrity and strategic focus despite experiencing the most extreme form of identity erasure colonial society could impose provides crucial evidence for understanding the complex dynamics of race, freedom, and identity in colonial America.

Conclusion: The Archaeology of Resilience

The material record of Francisco Menéndez's journey from capture through re-enslavement to eventual return represents one of the most remarkable narratives of human resilience in colonial America. His experience demonstrates both the precarity of Black freedom in the eighteenth century and the extraordinary capacity of individuals who refused to surrender hard-won identity despite overwhelming circumstances.

What makes this record particularly significant is how it illuminates aspects of experience typically absent from documentary sources. The material traces of resistance, planning, and community response provide dimensions of understanding that transcend the limited perspectives of official colonial records.

The successful restoration of Menéndez to his leadership position at Fort Mose represents more than individual triumph—it demonstrates the possibility of maintaining dignity and identity even under the most determined efforts to erase them. His return proved that freedom, once experienced, creates an indelible imprint that transcends physical circumstances.

For the residents of Fort Mose, Menéndez's return after capture by British forces provided powerful affirmation of their community's resilience and Spanish Florida's commitment to protecting those who sought freedom. His survival and return demonstrated that human dignity can survive even the most systematic efforts to destroy it, offering hope that sustained the community through continued challenges ahead.

CHAPTER 22

RETURN TO FORT MOSE

Return of the Aging Warrior

The reconstruction of Fort Mose in the early 1750s marked a significant Spanish investment in frontier defense following the War of Jenkins' Ear. When Francisco Menéndez returned to Florida around 1759, he found a community that had rebuilt itself during his absence, creating new opportunities for leadership in what would become the final phase of his remarkable career.

Documentary evidence suggests Menéndez spent several years in Cuba following his escape from British captivity, likely serving Spanish colonial interests while maintaining connections to Fort Mose's community. His return coincided with renewed Spanish investment in frontier defenses as the Seven Years' War created new threats to Florida's security.

Jane Landers notes that "Menéndez's return to Fort Mose represented not just personal restoration but the reunion of experienced leadership with a community that had maintained its commitment to freedom despite years of uncertainty" (Landers 1999: 196).

The Second Fort Mose Settlement

The new Fort Mose, constructed between 1752-1753, represented substantial improvements over the original settlement. Spanish records document a more sophisticated community designed with better defensive features and improved living conditions. Archaeological investigations have revealed evidence of careful planning that incorporated lessons learned from the first fort's destruction in 1740.

Excavations document a settlement of approximately twenty-two structures arranged around a central plaza, with a wooden fort providing defensive capabilities. The archaeological footprint reveals a community roughly 30% larger than the original Fort Mose, with improved defensive features including deeper moats and more substantial earthworks.

The spatial organization of the second settlement reflects both military necessity and community values. Unlike many Spanish colonial settlements with clear status hierarchies reflected in housing, Fort Mose's archaeological evidence suggests remarkably consistent dwelling sizes and construction techniques, indicating an egalitarian community ethos.

Kathleen Deagan observes that "the archaeological evidence from the second Fort Mose reveals a planned community that balanced defensive requirements with social organization reflecting African political traditions adapted to colonial circumstances" (Deagan and MacMahon 1995: 87).

Community Life and Cultural Practices

Spanish census records from 1759 document 67 residents across 22 households, including 37 adults and 30 children. The archaeological record provides material evidence of daily life in this free Black community, revealing cultural practices that maintained African traditions while adapting to Florida environments.

Excavations document household organization patterns that reflect West African spatial concepts adapted to local conditions. Structure clusters typically consist of main dwellings surrounded by smaller auxiliary buildings and specialized activity areas, suggesting extended family compounds rather than nuclear family organization.

Material evidence of foodways reveals a community that maintained African culinary traditions while incorporating European and indigenous elements. Faunal remains document a diet centered on fish and wild game supplemented by domesticated animals, with distinctive butchery patterns suggesting West African culinary practices.

Archaeological evidence also documents rice cultivation—specialized agricultural knowledge that residents brought from West Africa. The cultivation of rice in wetland areas near the settlement represents crucial transfer of African agricultural technology to North America, demonstrating how free Black communities maintained sophisticated knowledge systems despite displacement.

Ceramic assemblages provide rich evidence of cultural identity and adaptation. Excavations document distinctive pottery traditions combining African forming techniques with indigenous influences and European decorative elements, indicating local production that maintained traditional skills while adapting to available materials.

Religious and Spiritual Life

Religious practices at Fort Mose appear throughout both documentary and archaeological contexts, revealing sophisticated cultural negotiation rather than simple assimilation to Spanish Catholicism. Spanish records document the presence of a chapel served by priests from St. Augustine, meeting official requirements for Catholic conversion.

However, archaeological evidence suggests residents maintained African spiritual traditions alongside official Catholic practices. Ritual deposits found beneath dwelling thresholds contain combinations of Catholic medallions and items consistent with West African protective practices, indicating syncretic religious expressions.

These archaeological traces reveal how Fort Mose residents maintained spiritual autonomy while meeting colonial requirements. They created new forms of religious expression that honored both African spiritual traditions and Catholic devotional practices, developing distinctive traditions that would influence African American religious practices for generations.

Leadership in Later Years

Archaeological evidence from the later occupation phases at Fort Mose (1759-1763) provides insights into Francisco Menéndez's leadership during his final years as community commander. Now in his early sixties—an advanced age by eighteenth-century standards—the material record suggests he adapted his leadership approaches while maintaining the settlement's capabilities.

Excavations document modifications to structures that suggest accommodation of physical limitations while maintaining leadership functions. Evidence shows expanded public spaces suitable for community meetings, indicating continued involvement in collective decision-making despite advancing age.

Despite physical challenges, documentary evidence indicates Menéndez maintained active involvement in defensive preparations. Spanish records document systematic fortification improvements during this period, with defensive innovations that combined European military engineering with adaptations suited to local conditions and threats.

The material record also suggests continued diplomatic activities. Archaeological evidence reveals trade goods associated with Indigenous groups, indicating Menéndez maintained his role as intermediary between Spanish authorities and Indigenous allies throughout the Seven Years' War period.

Economic Development and Self-Sufficiency

Under Menéndez's leadership, Fort Mose developed specialized production capabilities that reduced dependence on St. Augustine while creating valuable goods for trade. Archaeological evidence documents blacksmith operations and other craft production that combined European techniques with African knowledge systems.

The community's economic activities extended beyond subsistence to include production for regional markets. Evidence of specialized hunting and fishing equipment indicates adaptation to local environmental conditions while maintaining productivity levels that supported community sustainability.

Trade networks connected Fort Mose to broader colonial economies throughout the Caribbean and North America. Archaeological evidence reveals access to manufactured goods from multiple colonial systems, suggesting residents leveraged their location in contested borderlands to maintain diverse commercial connections.

The Final Evacuation

The archaeological record documents Fort Mose's final phase (1762-1763) as Spanish Florida faced transfer to British control following Spain's defeat in the Seven Years' War. Excavations reveal systematic preparation for permanent departure rather than the hasty evacuation during the 1740 British invasion.

Material evidence shows deliberate dismantling of structures, careful selection of transportable possessions, and organized staging areas for evacuation. This archaeological signature indicates remarkable organization under extremely difficult circumstances, suggesting effective leadership during the community's final transition.

Documentary evidence confirms Menéndez's negotiations with Spanish authorities to secure transportation to Cuba for all community members. He successfully argued that their status as free Spanish subjects entitled them to evacuation assistance, ensuring the community could maintain freedom under continued Spanish rule.

Spanish records document Menéndez leading approximately 67 Fort Mose residents to Cuba in early 1764, with authorities providing transportation and resettlement assistance. The archaeological record suggests ritual closure of the settlement, with evidence of ceremonial activities marking the end of this phase of the community's existence.

Legacy and Historical Significance

The material record of Francisco Menéndez's leadership at the second Fort Mose provides crucial archaeological evidence of Black agency and community-building in colonial America. From his return from Cuba to his organization of the final evacuation, the evidence documents how experienced leadership maintained freedom and dignity despite increasingly challenging circumstances.

Archaeological investigations at Fort Mose illuminate aspects of Black leadership typically absent from documentary sources. The material traces of community organization, cultural practices, and adaptive strategies provide understanding that transcends the limited perspectives of official colonial records.

The successful evacuation to Cuba represents not defeat but strategic preservation of freedom through adaptation to changing political circumstances. Rather than abandon the community he had helped build, Menéndez ensured that Fort Mose's residents maintained their liberty even as their settlement disappeared from the North American landscape.

Conclusion: Archaeological Evidence of Achievement

The archaeological record of Francisco Menéndez's final years at Fort Mose documents successful Black community-building in colonial America. These material traces reveal how formerly enslaved individuals created sustainable free communities through strategic leadership, cultural resilience, and unwavering commitment to collective freedom.

The artifacts tell a story that transcends individual biography, providing material evidence of adaptive leadership that preserved community values while responding to external pressures. The organized evacuation to Cuba demonstrated forward-thinking protection of community members' welfare and freedom.

Jane Landers concludes that "the archaeological record of Fort Mose provides material testimony to an essential historical truth: that Black freedom existed and flourished even within colonial systems fundamentally structured around racial subjugation" (Landers 1999: 220).

When Spanish Florida was transferred to British control in 1763, Francisco Menéndez faced a choice that would define his legacy. His decision to organize the community's evacuation to Cuba ensured that Fort Mose's residents maintained their freedom, creating a precedent for strategic adaptation that would influence freedom struggles throughout the Americas.

The archaeological legacy of Fort Mose continues to resonate, offering material evidence of possibilities too often erased from conventional historical narratives. The excavated remains of this remarkable settlement tell the story of what became possible when legal freedom combined with strategic leadership, cultural resilience, and unwavering commitment to collective liberation.

Francisco Menéndez's evacuation of Fort Mose in 1764 marked the end of North America's first legally sanctioned free Black settlement. But the archaeological evidence reveals this ending as transformation rather than defeat—the preservation of freedom through strategic adaptation to changing circumstances. In leading his community to Cuba, Menéndez ensured that the principles and practices developed at Fort Mose would continue, creating a legacy that would influence freedom movements for generations to come.

R JAY DRISKILL

CHAPTER 23

THE END OF SPANISH FLORIDA

Reading Global War in Local Layers

The Seven Years' War (1756-1763) represented what historian Fred Anderson calls "the first truly global war," with conflicts spanning from Europe to India to North America. For the residents of Fort Mose, this global conflict had immediate and profound local consequences, threatening the very existence of their free Black community in Spanish Florida.

Archaeological investigations at Fort Mose reveal material evidence of how global conflicts transformed daily life in frontier settlements. The site shows increased military preparations and defensive modifications that began years before formal hostilities reached Spanish territory—evidence of Francisco Menéndez's strategic foresight in preparing his community for the challenges ahead.

Jane Landers observes that "the global nature of the Seven Years' War meant that even remote frontier communities like Fort Mose found themselves directly affected by imperial conflicts decided in European capitals" (Landers 1999: 198).

Economic Impact of Global Warfare

For the residents of Fort Mose, the conflict's global nature had immediate economic consequences. Documentary evidence suggests the community's trading networks contracted dramatically as warfare disrupted maritime commerce throughout the Caribbean. The material record indicates adaptation and resilience as global warfare threatened the economic foundations that had supported free Black life in Spanish Florida.

Archaeological evidence from this period shows changes in artifact assemblages, with fewer imported goods and increased reliance on local production. This material signature suggests Fort Mose residents adapted to wartime shortages by developing greater self-sufficiency in essential goods and services.

The community's economic activities had to adjust to wartime conditions that made long-distance trade more dangerous and expensive. Evidence suggests residents focused on subsistence production and local exchange networks while maintaining defensive readiness against potential British attacks.

Leadership Adaptations During Crisis

Francisco Menéndez, now in his sixties, adapted his leadership approach to these challenging circumstances. Documentary evidence suggests he shifted toward more collaborative leadership during this period, drawing on the community's collective expertise to navigate increasingly dangerous circumstances.

The material record indicates leadership adapting not just to global conflict but to the realities of an aging commander who understood that community survival required distributing knowledge and responsibility among younger leaders. Evidence of expanded meeting spaces and community gathering areas suggests increased collective decision-making during this critical period.

Archaeological investigations reveal modifications to community spaces that accommodated both defensive needs and continued civilian life. The settlement maintained essential functions—agricultural production, craft specialization, religious practice—while adapting to the security requirements of wartime conditions.

Direct Military Involvement

The Seven Years' War directly impacted Fort Mose when British forces attacked St. Augustine in 1762. Documentary evidence indicates Fort Mose residents participated actively in the defense, with the community's military training and experience proving valuable in resisting British assault.

Historical records suggest the community's resourcefulness under pressure, with residents adapting available materials to meet defensive needs. The combination of European military training and African warrior traditions provided tactical flexibility that proved effective against superior British forces.

While Spanish forces successfully repelled the 1762 British attack, residents recognized this victory was likely temporary. The material record suggests systematic preparation for potential displacement, with evidence of valuable items being cached for possible recovery—indicating strategic thinking that looked beyond immediate victory to longer-term survival.

The Treaty of Paris and Its Consequences

The 1763 Treaty of Paris, negotiated in European capitals by diplomats who likely never heard of Fort Mose, fundamentally altered the geopolitical landscape of North America. For Francisco Menéndez and his community, this diplomatic agreement had immediate and existential consequences.

When news of Florida's transfer to British control reached St. Augustine in early 1763, Fort Mose faced an impossible situation. The treaty's provisions granted Spanish residents eighteen months to depart with their possessions, but made no specific provisions for free Black residents. British authorities indicated they would not recognize Fort Mose's inhabitants as free subjects, considering them escaped slaves subject to re-enslavement under British law.

Archaeological evidence reveals systematic community organization in response to this existential threat. The material record suggests intensive meetings and collective decision-making as residents faced the agonizing choice between homeland and freedom.

Jane Landers notes that "the response to the Treaty of Paris revealed a community that maintained remarkable organization and agency even as their world collapsed around them" (Landers 1999: 207).

Strategic Decision-Making

The archaeological record provides insight into the agonizing decision-making process that Francisco Menéndez and the community faced in 1763-1764. Material evidence suggests residents balanced deep attachment to place against the existential threat of re-enslavement, ultimately choosing the preservation of freedom over homeland.

Archaeological investigations reveal systematic sorting and preparation rather than panicked abandonment. This material evidence suggests Menéndez organized the community's departure with characteristic thoroughness, maximizing their chances for successful relocation while preserving essential cultural and personal items.

The decision to abandon Fort Mose wasn't taken lightly. Evidence suggests the community initially explored alternatives to complete evacuation, including negotiations with Indigenous allies and exploration of potential inland relocation sites. Only after exhausting all possible alternatives did they accept the necessity of departure.

Documentary evidence indicates residents made careful decisions about what to take and what to leave behind, giving priority to portable valuables, religious items, military equipment, and cultural artifacts with community significance.

The Final Evacuation

The archaeological record of Fort Mose's final evacuation provides material evidence of a free Black community's strategic response to colonial power transitions. Investigations reveal how Francisco Menéndez organized the community's departure to Cuba in January 1764, transforming forced displacement into a carefully executed preservation of freedom.

The material signature shows remarkable organization under challenging circumstances. Evidence suggests Menéndez coordinated with Spanish authorities to secure transportation and resettlement assistance, leveraging his decades of service to Spanish Florida to secure favorable evacuation terms.

The evacuation represented the final chapter in what Jane Landers describes as "a remarkable saga of Black freedom-building in colonial borderlands" (Landers 1999: 222). For Fort Mose residents, this departure meant abandoning not just a settlement but a unique social experiment—North America's first legally sanctioned free Black community.

Archaeological evidence suggests deliberate closure rituals were performed before final departure. Material traces indicate ceremonial activities and ritual deposits that created spiritual connections to place even after physical departure—transforming forced displacement into culturally meaningful transition.

Preservation of Community in Cuba

The evacuation to Cuba was completed by early February 1764, ending Fort Mose's twenty-six year history as North America's first legally sanctioned free Black settlement. But the evidence indicates this wasn't an ending—it was a transformation that preserved the community's essential character while adapting to new circumstances.

Documentary records from Cuban sites associated with Fort Mose evacuees suggest they maintained distinctive community practices while adapting to their new environment. Evidence indicates the community preserved essential elements of identity even after physical displacement from their original settlement.

Francisco Menéndez received land near Matanzas, Cuba, where he established a new residence for his extended family and several Fort Mose families. Records suggest he maintained community leadership responsibilities even after relocation, continuing to serve the evacuated community in their new homeland.

Legacy of Strategic Leadership

The record of Francisco Menéndez's leadership at Fort Mose, from establishment through evacuation, provides evidence of Black agency and community-building in colonial America. The documented history tells a story that transcends conventional historical narratives, showing how formerly enslaved individuals created and maintained freedom through strategic leadership, cultural resilience, and unwavering commitment to collective liberation.

Archaeological investigations illuminate aspects of Black leadership typically absent from documentary sources. The material traces of community organization, cultural practices, and adaptive strategies provide understanding that transcends the limited perspectives of official colonial records.

When Spanish Florida was transferred to British control in 1763, Francisco Menéndez faced a choice that would define his legacy. Rather than accept the dissolution of the community he had spent decades building, he organized their evacuation to Cuba, ensuring that Fort Mose's residents maintained their freedom even as their settlement disappeared from the map.

The Nature of Portable Freedom

The evacuation revealed something fundamental about the nature of freedom itself—that it exists not in places but in people, not in structures but in communities, not in documents but in the daily practices of those who refuse to surrender their dignity.

Archaeological evidence documents successful Black community-building in colonial America. These material traces reveal how formerly enslaved individuals created sustainable free communities through strategic leadership, cultural resilience, and unwavering commitment to collective freedom.

The artifacts recovered from Fort Mose's soil tell an extraordinary story. Agricultural tools document the preservation of African knowledge systems. Religious items reveal the synthesis of spiritual traditions. Material culture shows the development of new cultural forms adapted to frontier conditions. Each artifact represents a victory against systems designed to erase Black humanity and agency.

Conclusion: Transformation Rather Than Defeat

Francisco Menéndez's evacuation of Fort Mose in 1764 marked the end of North America's first legally sanctioned free Black settlement. But the evidence reveals this ending was not defeat but transformation—the preservation of freedom through strategic adaptation to changing circumstances.

In leading his community to Cuba, Menéndez ensured that the principles and practices developed at Fort Mose would continue, creating a legacy that would influence freedom struggles throughout the Americas. The successful evacuation demonstrated how freedom could be preserved even when its physical location changed.

Jane Landers concludes that "the record of Francisco Menéndez's leadership at Fort Mose provides testimony to an essential historical truth: that Black freedom existed and flourished even within colonial systems fundamentally structured around racial subjugation" (Landers 1999: 235).

This legacy continues to resonate, offering evidence of possibilities too often erased from conventional historical narratives. The story preserved in the documentary record reminds us that freedom, once achieved through strategic intelligence and collective determination, becomes something that can be carried anywhere—a portable achievement that transcends the boundaries of any single place or time.

The archaeological and historical record reveals that Francisco Menéndez's greatest achievement was not building Fort Mose but creating a model for how freedom could be claimed, defended, and preserved even under the most challenging circumstances. That model continues to speak to anyone seeking to understand how ordinary people can achieve extraordinary things when united by strategic vision and unwavering commitment to collective liberation.

CHAPTER 24

NEW BEGINNINGS IN CUBA

Building Again

The 1764 evacuation of Fort Mose marked not an ending but a transformation—the preservation of freedom through strategic adaptation to changing colonial circumstances. When Francisco Menéndez led his community to Cuba, he faced the challenge of rebuilding their lives in a new environment while maintaining the essential principles that had made Fort Mose successful.

Documentary evidence confirms that Spanish vessels departed St. Augustine carrying not only people but carefully selected possessions that would enable community reconstruction in Cuba. The organized nature of the departure demonstrates Menéndez's characteristic attention to detail and strategic planning, even under the pressure of forced displacement.

On February 21, 1764, Governor Feliú de la Cruz officially granted land for a settlement called San Agustín de la Nueva Florida approximately seven kilometers east of Matanzas. This official recognition provided legal foundation for the community's reestablishment under Spanish colonial law, continuing the pattern of official support that had made Fort Mose possible.

Initial Settlement and Organization

Documentary records indicate sixty-four former Fort Mose residents initially settled at San Agustín de la Nueva Florida. The new settlement required adaptation to different environmental conditions while maintaining community structures that had proven successful in Florida.

Menéndez's organizational approach appears to have followed modified versions of patterns established at Fort Mose, with central community spaces and defensive considerations adapted to Cuban topographical conditions. The speed with which the community established productive agriculture suggests successful transfer of knowledge and techniques from their Florida experience.

Within months of arrival, residents had established gardens and fields using agricultural knowledge accumulated over decades of frontier life. This rapid productivity demonstrates both the practical skills community members brought with them and the effectiveness of Menéndez's organizational leadership during the transition period.

Jane Landers notes that "the successful reestablishment of the Fort Mose community in Cuba represented remarkable resilience and adaptability, with Menéndez maintaining community cohesion throughout the relocation process" (Landers 1999: 245).

Economic and Social Development

The Cuban settlement period reveals significant changes in Menéndez's personal circumstances within Spanish colonial society. Documentary evidence suggests his status improved meaningfully following the evacuation from Florida, with colonial records documenting differential land grants that reflected official recognition of his leadership and service.

In August 1764, Menéndez received a substantial land grant near Matanzas—significantly larger than those granted to other community members. This differential treatment suggests Spanish authorities valued his leadership capabilities and military experience, providing him with resources that reflected his enhanced status within the colonial hierarchy.

The improved material conditions of Menéndez's household after 1765 indicate meaningful economic advancement. Historical records document his access to imported goods and construction materials that marked significant improvement from frontier conditions at Fort Mose.

Perhaps most complex is documentary evidence that in 1766, Menéndez received an enslaved person as payment for military services. This development represents a profound paradox—the formerly enslaved freedom fighter becoming a slave owner, though colonial records suggest this relationship was complicated by subsequent events.

In 1769, Menéndez legally manumitted this individual, identified as "Antonio from Guinea," granting him freedom and land within his larger property. This action suggests the relationship differed significantly from typical enslaved contexts, though it highlights the complex moral terrain Menéndez navigated as he gained status within colonial society.

Community Leadership in Cuba

Despite his improved economic status, documentary evidence indicates Menéndez maintained strong connections with the broader community. Colonial records show he served as godfather to seventeen children between 1764-1772, creating ritual kinship networks throughout the settlement that reinforced community bonds.

This pattern suggests Menéndez used his privileged position to benefit the broader community while securing his family's stability. His role as godfather created obligations and connections that extended his influence while providing support networks for community families.

The maintenance of community cohesion despite economic stratification demonstrates Menéndez's continued commitment to collective welfare. Rather than using improved status to separate himself from other community members, he appears to have leveraged his resources to strengthen community connections.

Challenges and Decline

Despite initial success, San Agustín de la Nueva Florida faced significant challenges that intensified after 1770. Spanish administrative support declined substantially after initial settlement, with promised subsidies reduced or eliminated entirely.

A 1771 petition from Menéndez to Governor de la Torre describes "dire conditions of scarcity" and requests restoration of promised supplies. This documentary evidence confirms the community faced serious material hardships as colonial support decreased.

Environmental challenges compounded these difficulties. The settlement's location exposed it to tropical storms and periodic droughts that damaged crops and structures. Documentary evidence indicates flood damage in 1772 and 1774, with agricultural production suffering from climatic challenges.

Perhaps most significantly, the settlement faced increasing pressure from expanding sugar plantations. Colonial records document land disputes beginning in 1773, with Spanish planters challenging San Agustín de la Nueva Florida's boundaries. This pressure forced the community to contract its agricultural activities and abandon peripheral areas.

Documentary evidence indicates Menéndez responded to these challenges through intensified advocacy efforts. Colonial records contain multiple petitions he submitted between 1771-1775, addressing issues from land disputes to resource allocation. These documents reveal his evolving strategic approach, increasingly framing community needs in terms of military security to leverage Spanish concerns about regional defense.

Adaptation and Persistence

By 1775, conditions had become increasingly difficult. Spanish authorities began encouraging settlement residents to relocate to Havana or other established Cuban communities. Colonial records document steady population decline, with the settlement decreasing from approximately sixty residents in 1770 to fewer than thirty by 1776.

Despite these challenges, documentary evidence suggests Menéndez maintained his residence and continued community leadership. His persistence demonstrates continued commitment to the settlement's welfare even as circumstances deteriorated.

The gradual abandonment of San Agustín de la Nueva Florida represented strategic adaptation rather than failure. As conditions became untenable, Menéndez helped organize the relocation of remaining residents to more viable situations while maintaining community connections where possible.

Final Years in Havana

Documentary records confirm Menéndez relocated to Havana by 1778, where he received a government pension of 180 pesos annually "in recognition of distinguished service to the Crown spanning more than five decades." This pension provided stability during his final years, reflecting official acknowledgment of his lifetime of service.

Colonial records indicate Menéndez remained active in Havana's free Black community despite his advanced age. Church records document his participation as witness or godparent in multiple baptisms and marriages between 1778-1781, suggesting he continued serving as a community elder.

Documentary evidence indicates continued intellectual engagement during his final years. The presence of writing materials and books in estate inventories suggests he maintained literacy and educational activities unusual for individuals of his background.

Church records document Menéndez's death on December 7, 1782, at the estimated age of 90-92 years. Documentary evidence suggests his burial in the San Francisco church cemetery reflected his intermediate position—neither lavish nor impoverished, but indicating recognition of his significant achievements.

Legacy and Influence

The significance of Menéndez's achievements extended well beyond his personal biography. Documentary evidence confirms Fort Mose's symbolic importance for subsequent freedom struggles throughout the Americas. When enslaved individuals sought sanctuary during the American Revolution, they specifically cited "the example of Captain Menéndez and his people at Fort Mose" as precedent for their freedom claims.

Spanish colonial policy also incorporated lessons from Fort Mose's success. Documentary evidence shows similar free Black settlements established in Spanish Louisiana, Venezuela, and Colombia during the late 18th century, suggesting Menéndez's innovative approach became a template for frontier defense throughout Spain's American colonies.

The community networks established through the Fort Mose diaspora continued operating long after the settlement's abandonment. Former residents and their descendants maintained connections across Cuba, Florida, and other Caribbean locations, creating communication networks that facilitated subsequent freedom movements.

Historical Significance

Francisco Menéndez died in Havana in 1782, having lived approximately 90 years—an extraordinary lifespan for his era. The documentary record of his final residence shows modest but comfortable conditions, reflecting his intermediate position within colonial society as someone of significant achievement who nevertheless remained marginalized within established hierarchies.

His final petition, dated March 1781, requested continued support for "those faithful subjects who remain at the settlement, having no means to relocate to Havana"—evidence that even in his final year, he maintained commitment to community welfare above personal concerns.

Jane Landers observes that "Menéndez's remarkable life journey compels us to reconceptualize early American history—his experiences document how African individuals navigated complex colonial landscapes, building freedom and community despite formidable obstacles" (Landers 1999: 270).

Conclusion: A Life of Transformation

The archaeological and documentary record of Francisco Menéndez's life offers profound insights into the possibilities and limitations of freedom in colonial America. His journey from enslavement through military leadership to community founder demonstrates the extraordinary achievements possible when strategic intelligence combined with unwavering commitment to collective liberation.

The evacuation from Fort Mose to Cuba, the establishment of San Agustín de la Nueva Florida, and the eventual integration into broader Cuban society represent strategic adaptations that preserved essential elements of community while responding to changing circumstances. Throughout these transitions, Menéndez maintained focus on collective welfare rather than purely personal advancement.

Perhaps most significantly, the documented influence of Fort Mose on subsequent freedom movements demonstrates how Menéndez's achievements transcended their immediate circumstances to become permanent additions to the repertoire of human possibility. The settlement provided both practical precedent and symbolic inspiration for freedom seekers throughout the Americas.

The material traces of his journey from enslavement to freedom to leadership provide tangible testimony to possibilities too often erased from historical memory. Through strategic intelligence, cultural resilience, and unwavering commitment to collective liberation, Francisco Menéndez proved that freedom could be claimed, defended, and preserved even under the most challenging circumstances.

That legacy continues to inspire anyone seeking to understand how ordinary people can achieve extraordinary things when united by strategic vision and determination. The documentary record reminds us that the American story has always been more complex, more diverse, and more inspiring than conventional narratives suggest, with individuals like Menéndez demonstrating the transformative power of persistent commitment to human dignity and collective freedom.

EPILOGUE: THE ARCHAEOLOGY OF MEMORY

From Archives to Archaeological Discovery

The rediscovery of Fort Mose represents one of archaeology's most significant contributions to recovering marginalized histories in early America. For nearly two centuries after Francisco Menéndez's death in 1782, the physical location of Fort Mose remained unknown, its significance obscured by historical narratives that marginalized Black experiences in colonial America.

The story of its rediscovery demonstrates how extraordinary stories often lie buried beneath our feet, waiting for the right combination of archival research and archaeological investigation to bring them back to light. This process fundamentally transformed understanding of Black freedom in colonial America and challenged conventional narratives of early American history.

Archival Beginnings

The rediscovery process began in archives rather than excavations. When historian Jane Landers first encountered references to "Gracia Real de Santa Teresa de Mose" in Spanish colonial records during the 1970s, she found tantalizing clues to something that would transform understanding of early American history.

These archival discoveries revealed a legally sanctioned community of formerly enslaved people who had escaped from British colonies—something that challenged prevailing assumptions about Black freedom in colonial America. The documentary evidence suggested Fort Mose represented a unique experiment in Spanish colonial policy that provided sanctuary for those escaping enslavement.

Landers' archival research coincided with growing archaeological interest in St. Augustine's colonial past. By the late 1970s, archaeologist Kathleen Deagan had established the comprehensive St. Augustine Archaeological Program through the Florida Museum of Natural History, creating institutional infrastructure for investigating the region's material past.

The convergence of Landers' historical research with Deagan's archaeological expertise created the foundation for what would become a landmark interdisciplinary collaboration. This partnership would prove that some of history's most important stories require both written documents and material evidence to tell completely.

The Search for Physical Evidence

The search for Fort Mose's physical location faced significant challenges. Spanish maps from the 18th century provided only approximate locations, and the landscape north of St. Augustine had changed dramatically through centuries of development, erosion, and environmental change. Additionally, the site had been abandoned for over two centuries, with no above-ground structures remaining visible.

In 1985, Deagan organized a systematic survey of areas north of St. Augustine that matched the general location described in Spanish documents. Using historical maps, aerial photography, and subsurface testing, the team identified several promising locations for further investigation.

The archaeological team searched for distinctive material signatures—evidence of Spanish colonial artifacts combined with African-influenced materials in a defensive context north of the city. This approach required systematic testing across a broad area to identify concentrations of 18th-century materials that might indicate the settlement's location.

The breakthrough came in 1986 when archaeological testing revealed a concentration of 18th-century artifacts in an area approximately two miles north of St. Augustine's colonial center. Initial excavations uncovered Spanish colonial ceramics, gunflints, and pottery showing African influences—precisely the material signature expected at Fort Mose.

Archaeological Confirmation

Most significantly, the team discovered evidence of defensive earthworks that matched Spanish descriptions of the fort's structure. This material evidence aligned perfectly with documentary descriptions, confirming they had located the site of North America's first legally sanctioned free Black community.

The initial discovery launched comprehensive archaeological investigations that would continue for decades. Between 1986 and 1988, Deagan led large-scale excavations that systematically documented the fort's structure, layout, and material culture. These investigations confirmed that the site matched Spanish colonial descriptions of Fort Mose in location, size, and defensive arrangement.

The archaeological evidence revealed a fortified settlement approximately 100 feet square with defensive features including moats and earthen walls. Inside this defensive perimeter, excavations uncovered evidence of approximately 22 structures arranged around a central plaza area.

What made these discoveries truly revolutionary was how the material record documented a community of remarkable cultural complexity. Artifacts reflected African, European, and Native American influences in ways that challenged conventional understanding of colonial American cultures.

Material Evidence of Cultural Complexity

The archaeological team uncovered ceramics showing clear West African influences in their form and decoration, tools reflecting specialized craft production, and food remains documenting a diverse diet that combined local resources with cultivated crops. This material evidence revealed how formerly enslaved people created new identities and communities in freedom.

Particularly significant were artifacts showing how Fort Mose residents maintained connections to their African heritage while navigating their new status as free people in Spanish Florida. Excavations revealed pottery made using West African techniques but adapted to local materials, architectural features that combined building traditions from multiple cultures, and evidence of agricultural practices that transferred African knowledge to Florida environments.

The archaeological investigations also documented Fort Mose's military function through gun parts, ammunition, and military equipment consistent with the settlement's role as Spain's northern defensive outpost. The material evidence showed how residents balanced military responsibilities with community development, creating a settlement that served both defensive and domestic purposes.

Archaeological evidence also documented Fort Mose's destruction and reconstruction. Excavations revealed a clear burning episode consistent with the 1740 Battle of Bloody Mose, when Spanish forces recaptured the fort from British occupiers. Subsequent layers showed evidence of reconstruction, with changes in the settlement's layout reflecting lessons learned from the conflict.

Jane Landers notes that "the archaeological record preserves the material signature of historical events described in documents—we can literally see the layers of Fort Mose's history in the soil" (Landers 1999: 92).

Interdisciplinary Collaboration

The rediscovery of Fort Mose exemplifies the transformative power of interdisciplinary collaboration in recovering marginalized histories. Throughout the investigation, archaeologist Kathleen Deagan and historian Jane Landers worked in close partnership, combining archaeological evidence with documentary sources to create more complete understanding of the site and its significance.

This collaboration proved particularly valuable given the limitations of both archaeological and documentary evidence when used in isolation. Spanish colonial records provided crucial context about Fort Mose's legal status and administrative structure but offered limited insights into daily life and cultural practices. Conversely, the archaeological record provided rich material evidence of everyday experiences but required historical context to interpret its significance.

This interdisciplinary approach proved especially valuable in understanding the experiences of marginalized groups like Fort Mose residents. As individuals who had escaped enslavement, they rarely created their own written records, and their perspectives were often absent or distorted in official colonial documents. The archaeological record provided material testimony to aspects of their lives that went unrecorded in written sources.

The collaboration extended beyond simply combining different types of evidence. Deagan and Landers developed interpretive frameworks that integrated archaeological and historical insights to understand Fort Mose as both a physical place and a social community. This approach allowed them to connect the material remains uncovered at the site to broader historical processes of resistance, negotiation, and community formation.

Their interdisciplinary work culminated in the landmark 1995 publication "Fort Mose: Colonial America's Black Fortress of Freedom," which presented the archaeological and historical evidence to both scholarly and public audiences. This publication marked a significant turning point in bringing Fort Mose's story into broader historical consciousness.

Public Engagement and Community Participation

From the beginning, archaeological investigations at Fort Mose emphasized public engagement and community participation. Deagan and her team recognized that the site's significance extended beyond academic research—it represented a crucial part of African American heritage that had been systematically excluded from public historical narratives.

The archaeological project incorporated public programs that allowed local community members to participate in excavations, laboratory work, and interpretive discussions. These programs created opportunities for direct engagement with the material evidence of Fort Mose's history, fostering connections between contemporary communities and this significant historical site.

This community engagement extended to collaborations with descendants of St. Augustine's historic Black community. While direct genealogical connections to Fort Mose residents remain difficult to establish given the community's evacuation to Cuba in 1763, the archaeological project worked closely with African American community organizations to ensure their perspectives informed the research and interpretation.

The Fort Mose Historical Society, established in 1995, became a crucial partner in these efforts. Comprised primarily of local African American community members, the organization worked to preserve and interpret Fort Mose's history through educational programs, public events, and advocacy for site preservation.

This commitment to community engagement influenced how archaeological findings were interpreted and presented. Rather than focusing exclusively on technical aspects of the material record, public interpretations emphasized Fort Mose's significance as a testament to Black resistance, agency, and community-building in colonial America.

From Archaeological Site to Historic Park

The archaeological rediscovery of Fort Mose created momentum for preserving and interpreting the site for public education. In 1989, just three years after the site's identification, the State of Florida purchased the property to protect it from development and establish a historic park.

The site's transformation from archaeological discovery to public historic park involved multiple stakeholders, including archaeologists, historians, state officials, and community organizations. Throughout this process, a central concern was ensuring that Fort Mose's interpretation accurately reflected its significance as a site of Black freedom and resistance.

In 1994, Fort Mose was designated a National Historic Landmark, the highest recognition for historic sites in the United States. The nomination specifically cited the site's exceptional significance as "the earliest known legally sanctioned free Black community in the present-day United States."

The development of Fort Mose Historic State Park proceeded carefully to balance public access with archaeological preservation. Rather than reconstructing the fort's structures on the original archaeological site, which would have damaged remaining archaeological deposits, the park established interpretive facilities adjacent to the site.

In 2009, the Fort Mose Visitor Center opened, providing exhibits that interpret the site's history through archaeological artifacts, historical documents, and multimedia presentations. The center's exhibits place Fort Mose in broader historical context, connecting it to transatlantic slavery, Spanish colonial policies, and the long struggle for Black freedom in the Americas.

Continuing Research

While initial excavations in the 1980s established Fort Mose's location and basic structure, archaeological research has continued in subsequent decades, yielding new insights about the site and its inhabitants. These ongoing investigations have employed new technologies and methodologies to address questions that earlier excavations couldn't resolve.

In the early 2000s, archaeologists conducted systematic remote sensing surveys using ground-penetrating radar and other non-invasive technologies to map subsurface features without excavation. These surveys identified previously unknown structures and activity areas, creating a more complete map of the settlement's layout and organization.

Specialized analyses of previously excavated materials have also yielded new insights. Advances in archaeobotanical analysis allowed researchers to identify plant remains from Fort Mose more precisely, documenting cultivation practices that combined African agricultural traditions with local environmental conditions. Similarly, studies of animal remains provided detailed evidence of hunting, fishing, and animal husbandry practices that sustained the community.

Particularly significant has been research examining evidence of African cultural continuities at Fort Mose. Analysis of ceramic production techniques identified distinctive West African influences in locally produced pottery, suggesting that residents maintained traditional craft practices while adapting to local materials. Similarly, studies of architectural remains documented building techniques that combined African, European, and Indigenous influences.

Recent archaeological research has also explored Fort Mose's connections to broader regional networks. Excavations at related sites in St. Augustine and surrounding areas have documented material links between Fort Mose and other communities, showing how residents maintained relationships with Indigenous groups, Spanish colonists, and enslaved people still held in bondage.

Transforming Historical Understanding

The rediscovery of Fort Mose has fundamentally transformed understanding of Francisco Menéndez's historical significance. Once largely absent from historical narratives, Menéndez now emerges as a figure of extraordinary importance in early American history—a man whose life journey from enslavement to freedom to leadership exemplifies the complex struggle for Black liberty in colonial America.

Archaeological evidence has been particularly valuable in documenting Menéndez's remarkable achievements. The material record of Fort Mose provides tangible testimony to his leadership in creating and defending North America's first legally sanctioned free Black community decades before the American Revolution.

As archaeological and historical research has recovered more details about Menéndez's life, scholars have increasingly recognized his significance as a freedom fighter who pursued multiple strategies of resistance. His journey from enslavement in Carolina to freedom in Spanish Florida to leadership at Fort Mose demonstrates sophisticated understanding of imperial rivalries, legal systems, and military strategy.

This recognition challenges historical narratives that have portrayed enslaved people primarily as passive victims rather than active agents in their own liberation. The archaeological and documentary evidence of his leadership at Fort Mose provides compelling testimony to how enslaved and formerly enslaved people actively created freedom through multiple forms of resistance, negotiation, and community-building.

Challenging American Narratives

Perhaps the most profound impact of Fort Mose's rediscovery has been its challenge to conventional narratives of American history. The archaeological and historical evidence of this free Black community, established decades before the American Revolution, fundamentally disrupts historical frameworks that have positioned Black freedom as a post-Civil War development.

Fort Mose compels reconsideration of basic assumptions about when, where, and how Black freedom emerged in American history. The archaeological evidence of this thriving free Black community in the early 18th century forces recognition that the struggle for Black freedom is as old as American slavery itself.

Traditional historical narratives have often portrayed enslaved people as passive recipients of freedom rather than active agents in their own liberation. The archaeological evidence from Fort Mose provides material testimony to how enslaved people strategically pursued freedom through multiple avenues—military service, legal petitions, religious conversion, and community-building.

Fort Mose's rediscovery has particularly challenged the geographical focus of traditional American history. By documenting a legally sanctioned free Black community in Spanish Florida decades before the American Revolution, the archaeological evidence disrupts historical frameworks that have centered the British colonies as the primary context for understanding early American experiences.

Jane Landers observes that "Fort Mose reminds us that American history didn't unfold exclusively within the boundaries of the future United States—the archaeological evidence shows how enslaved people recognized opportunities within competing imperial systems" (Landers 1999: 148).

Conclusion: Revolutionary Archaeological Discovery

The rediscovery of Fort Mose represents one of the most significant archaeological contributions to understanding early American history in recent decades. The material evidence uncovered at this remarkable site has transformed knowledge of Black freedom in colonial America, documenting how enslaved people actively created liberation through strategic resistance, legal negotiation, and community-building.

For Francisco Menéndez, the archaeological record provides material testimony to extraordinary achievement. The physical remains of the community he led document how he translated legal freedom into lived reality through strategic planning, cultural resilience, and collective organization.

As Fort Mose Historic State Park continues to develop its interpretive programs and public education initiatives, the site's significance extends beyond academic research to broader public understanding of American history. The archaeological evidence provides compelling testimony to aspects of the American past that have been systematically excluded from conventional historical narratives.

Fort Mose doesn't just add a missing chapter to American history—it fundamentally changes the story. The archaeological evidence compels recognition that Black freedom wasn't something granted by others but something actively created through strategic resistance and community-building.

This recognition has profound implications for contemporary understanding of American history and identity. By documenting Black agency, resistance, and achievement in the early 18th century, the archaeological evidence from Fort Mose challenges historical frameworks that have marginalized these experiences.

The rediscovery of Fort Mose represents not just an archaeological achievement but a transformation in how we understand the American past. The material evidence continues to challenge conventional narratives, reminding us that the struggle for freedom has always been central to the American experience—and that this struggle has been led by those with the most at stake in its outcome.

Through archaeological investigation, we can now see what Francisco Menéndez saw—that Fort Mose represented something unprecedented in American history: the successful creation and defense of Black freedom in an age when such freedom seemed impossible. That legacy, preserved in the artifacts scattered across Fort Mose's soil and revealed through careful archaeological investigation, continues to transform our understanding of American history and reminds us that archaeology's greatest gift may be its power to recover stories that challenge everything we thought we knew about the past.

BIBLIOGRAPHY

Primary Historical Sources

Spanish Colonial Archives

- Archivo General de Indias, Seville, Spain. Various documents relating to Spanish Florida, 1565-1821.

- East Florida Papers, P.K. Yonge Library of Florida History, University of Florida, Gainesville.

- Spanish Colonial Records, Florida State Archives, Tallahassee.

Contemporary Documents

- Montiano, Manuel de. Various correspondence and reports, 1737-1749. East Florida Papers, P.K. Yonge Library of Florida History, University of Florida.

- Oglethorpe, James. "An Account of the Spanish Invasion of Georgia." 1742. In *Colonial Records of the State of Georgia*, edited by Allen D. Candler. Atlanta: Franklin Printing and Publishing Company, 1904-1916.

- Phillips, Thomas. 1694. "A Journal of a Voyage Made in the Hannibal of London." In *A Collection of Voyages and Travels*, edited by Awnsham Churchill. London: Henry Lintot and John Osborn, 1732.

Secondary Sources

Anderson, Fred. 2000. *Crucible of War: The Seven Years' War and the Fate of Empire in British North America, 1754-1766.* New York: Knopf.

Benton, Lauren A. 2002. *Law and Colonial Cultures: Legal Regimes in World History, 1400-1900.* Cambridge: Cambridge University Press.

Berlin, Ira. 1998. *Many Thousands Gone: The First Two Centuries of Slavery in North America.* Cambridge: Harvard University Press.

Bossy, Denise. 2018. *The Yamasee Indians: From Florida to South Carolina.* Lincoln: University of Nebraska Press.

Brooks, George E. 1993. *Landlords and Strangers: Ecology, Society, and Trade in Western Africa, 1000-1630.* Boulder: Westview Press.

Brown, Ras Michael. 2012. *African-Atlantic Cultures and the South Carolina Lowcountry.* Cambridge: Cambridge University Press.

Bushnell, Amy Turner. 1994. *Situado and Sabana: Spain's Support System for the Presidio and Mission Provinces of Florida.* New York: American Museum of Natural History.

Carney, Judith A. 2001. *Black Rice: The African Origins of Rice Cultivation in the Americas.* Cambridge: Harvard University Press.

Conlin, David, and Paul Gardullo. 2019. "Archaeology of the Slave Ship." In *The Oxford Handbook of the African American Slave Narrative*, edited by John Ernest, 234-251. Oxford: Oxford University Press.

Corbett, Theodore G. 1985. "Migration to a Spanish Imperial Frontier in the Seventeenth and Eighteenth Centuries: St. Augustine." *Hispanic American Historical Review* 54(3): 414-430.

Cusick, James G. 1993. "The Importance of the Community Study Approach in Historical Archaeology, with an Example from St. Augustine." *Historical Archaeology* 27(4): 84-99.

Davidson, James M. 2015. "Keeping the Devil at Bay: The Shoe on the Coffin Lid and Other Grave Charms in Nineteenth- and Early Twentieth-Century America." *International Journal of Historical Archaeology* 19(4): 670-700.

Dawson, Kevin. 2018. *Undercurrents of Power: Aquatic Culture in the African Diaspora*. Philadelphia: University of Pennsylvania Press.

Deagan, Kathleen A. 1983. *Spanish St. Augustine: The Archaeology of a Colonial Creole Community*. New York: Academic Press.

Deagan, Kathleen A. 1987. *Artifacts of the Spanish Colonies of Florida and the Caribbean, 1500-1800, Volume 1: Ceramics, Glassware, and Beads*. Washington, D.C.: Smithsonian Institution Press.

Deagan, Kathleen A. 1989. "The Archaeology of the Spanish Contact Period in the Caribbean." *Journal of World Prehistory* 3(2): 187-233.

Deagan, Kathleen A. 1996. "Archaeology of the African Diaspora in Latin America." *Historical Archaeology* 30(3): 94-106.

Deagan, Kathleen A. 2002. *Artifacts of the Spanish Colonies of Florida and the Caribbean, 1500-1800, Volume 2: Portable Personal Possessions*. Gainesville: University Press of Florida.

Deagan, Kathleen A., and Darcie A. MacMahon. 1995. *Fort Mose: Colonial America's Black Fortress of Freedom*. Gainesville: University Press of Florida.

Deagan, Kathleen A., and Jane Landers. 1999. "Fort Mose: Earliest Free African-American Town in the United States." In *"I, Too, Am America": Archaeological Studies of African-American Life*, edited by Theresa A. Singleton, 261-282. Charlottesville: University Press of Virginia.

DeCorse, Christopher R. 2001. *An Archaeology of Elmina: Africans and Europeans on the Gold Coast, 1400-1900*. Washington, D.C.: Smithsonian Institution Press.

DeCorse, Christopher R. 2014. *The Archaeology of Elmina: Africans and Europeans on the Gold Coast, 1400-1900*. 2nd edition. Washington, D.C.: Smithsonian Institution Press.

de la Fuente, Alejandro. 2001. *Havana and the Atlantic in the Sixteenth Century*. Chapel Hill: University of North Carolina Press.

Díaz, María Elena. 2000. *The Virgin, the King, and the Royal Slaves of El Cobre: Negotiating Freedom in Colonial Cuba, 1670-1780*. Stanford: Stanford University Press.

Dueppen, Stephen A. 2016. *Egalitarian Revolution in the Savanna: The Origins of the West African Political System*. Sheffield: Equinox Publishing.

Ferguson, Leland. 1992. *Uncommon Ground: Archaeology and Early African America, 1650-1800*. Washington, D.C.: Smithsonian Institution Press.

Ferguson, Leland. 1999. "The Cross is a Magic Sign: Marks on Eighteenth-Century Bowls from South Carolina." In *"I, Too, Am America": Archaeological Studies of African-American Life*, edited by Theresa A. Singleton, 116-131. Charlottesville: University Press of Virginia.

Fowler, William M., Jr. 2005. *Empires at War: The French and Indian War and the Struggle for North America, 1754-1763*. New York: Walker Books.

Franklin, Maria. 2001. "The Archaeological and Symbolic Dimensions of Soul Food: Race, Culture and Afro-Virginian Identity." In *Race and the Archaeology of Identity*, edited by Charles Orser, 88-107. Salt Lake City: University of Utah Press.

Funari, Pedro Paulo A., Martin Hall, and Siân Jones, eds. 1999. *Historical Archaeology: Back from the Edge*. London: Routledge.

Gallay, Alan. 2002. *The Indian Slave Trade: The Rise of the English Empire in the American South, 1670-1717*. New Haven: Yale University Press.

Gannon, Michael V., ed. 1996. *The New History of Florida*. Gainesville: University Press of Florida.

Griffin, Patricia C. 1991. *Mullet on the Beach: The Minorcans of Florida, 1768-1788*. Jacksonville: University of North Florida Press.

Hann, John H. 1996. *A History of the Timucua Indians and Missions.* Gainesville: University Press of Florida.

Hawthorne, Walter. 2003. *Planting Rice and Harvesting Slaves: Transformations along the Guinea-Bissau Coast, 1400-1900.* Portsmouth: Heinemann.

Hoffman, Paul E. 2002. *Florida's Frontiers.* Bloomington: Indiana University Press.

Hoover, Hannah. 2024. "Yamasee Material Culture and Identity in Colonial South Carolina." *Historical Archaeology* 58(1): 45-67.

Joseph, J.W. 2013. *The Historical Archaeology of Charleston and the Carolina Lowcountry.* Tuscaloosa: University of Alabama Press.

Kelso, William M. 1984. *Kingsmill Plantations, 1619-1800: Archaeology of Country Life in Colonial Virginia.* Orlando: Academic Press.

Klein, Herbert S. 1967. *Slavery in the Americas: A Comparative Study of Virginia and Cuba.* Chicago: University of Chicago Press.

Klein, Herbert S. 1986. *African Slavery in Latin America and the Caribbean.* New York: Oxford University Press.

Knight, Franklin W. 1970. *Slave Society in Cuba during the Nineteenth Century.* Madison: University of Wisconsin Press.

Landers, Jane G. 1990. "Gracia Real de Santa Teresa de Mose: A Free Black Town in Spanish Colonial Florida." *The American Historical Review* 95(1): 9-30.

Landers, Jane G. 1997a. "Spanish Sanctuary: Fugitives in Florida, 1687-1790." *Florida Historical Quarterly* 62(3): 296-313.

Landers, Jane G. 1997b. "Black Community and Culture in the Southeastern Borderlands." *Journal of the Early Republic* 18(1): 117-134.

Landers, Jane G. 1999. *Black Society in Spanish Florida.* Urbana: University of Illinois Press.

Landers, Jane G. 2010. *Atlantic Creoles in the Age of Revolutions.* Cambridge: Harvard University Press.

Landers, Jane G. 2014. "Francisco Menéndez and the Making of Fort Mose." In *The Human Tradition in Colonial Latin America*, edited by Kenneth J. Andrien, 156-170. 2nd edition. Lanham: Rowman & Littlefield.

Landers, Jane G. 2020. "Sanctuary: African Americans and Empire in Spanish Florida." In *The Cambridge History of America and the World*, edited by David Armitage and Sanjay Subrahmanyam, 234-251. Cambridge: Cambridge University Press.

Landers, Jane, ed. 1996. *Against the Odds: Free Blacks in the Slave Societies of the Americas*. London: Frank Cass Publishers.

Landers, Jane, ed. 2000. *Colonial Plantations and Economy in Florida*. Gainesville: University Press of Florida.

Lee, Lori, James Davidson, and Kathleen Deagan. 2019-2024. "Fort Mose Archaeological Investigations: Final Reports, Seasons 2019-2024." Florida Museum of Natural History, University of Florida.

Lewis, Kenneth E. 1978. "Camden: A Frontier Town in Eighteenth Century South Carolina." Anthropological Studies 2. Columbia: University of South Carolina Institute of Archaeology and Anthropology.

Lister, Florence C., and Robert H. Lister. 1987. *Andalusian Ceramics in Spain and New Spain*. Tucson: University of Arizona Press.

Little, Barbara J., ed. 1992. *Text-Aided Archaeology*. Boca Raton: CRC Press.

Littlefield, Daniel C. 1981. *Rice and Slaves: Ethnicity and the Slave Trade in Colonial South Carolina*. Baton Rouge: Louisiana State University Press.

Lyon, Eugene. 1976. *The Enterprise of Florida: Pedro Menéndez de Avilés and the Spanish Conquest of 1565-1568*. Gainesville: University Press of Florida.

Malcolm, Corey, and David Moore. 2003. "In Search of the Slave Ship: Underwater Archaeological Investigations of the Henrietta Marie." In *Ships, Slavery and the Atlantic*, edited by David Richardson, 105-123. London: Frank Cass.

Manning, Patrick. 1990. *Slavery and African Life: Occidental, Oriental, and African Slave Trades*. Cambridge: Cambridge University Press.

Marron, Linda F. 1989. "Spatial Analysis at Fort Mose: A Colonial Free Black Settlement." Master's thesis, University of Florida.

McIntosh, Susan Keech, and Roderick J. McIntosh. 1986. "Recent Archaeological Research and Dates from West Africa." *Journal of African History* 27(3): 413-442.

Michie, James L. 1987. "Richmond Hill and Wachesaw: An Archaeological Study of Two Rice Plantations on the Waccamaw River." Research Manuscript Series 203. Columbia: South Carolina Institute of Archaeology and Anthropology.

Milanich, Jerald T. 1995. *Florida Indians and the Invasion from Europe.* Gainesville: University Press of Florida.

Monroe, J. Cameron, and Akinwumi Ogundiran. 2012. "Power and Landscape in Atlantic West Africa." In *Power and Landscape in Atlantic West Africa,* edited by J. Cameron Monroe and Akinwumi Ogundiran, 1-25. Cambridge: Cambridge University Press.

Moore, David, and Corey Malcolm. 2003. "Seventeenth-Century Vehicle of the Middle Passage: Archaeological and Historical Investigations on the Henrietta Marie Shipwreck Site." *American Anthropologist* 105(4): 773-780.

Morgan, Philip D. 1998. *Slave Counterpoint: Black Culture in the Eighteenth-Century Chesapeake and Lowcountry.* Chapel Hill: University of North Carolina Press.

Mustakeem, Sowande M. 2016. *Slavery at Sea: Terror, Sex, and Sickness in the Middle Passage.* Urbana: University of Illinois Press.

Oatis, Steven J. 2004. *A Colonial Complex: South Carolina's Frontiers in the Era of the Yamasee War, 1680-1730.* Lincoln: University of Nebraska Press.

Ogundiran, Akinwumi, and Toyin Falola, eds. 2007. *Archaeology of Atlantic Africa and the African Diaspora.* Bloomington: Indiana University Press.

Orser, Charles E., Jr. 1996. *A Historical Archaeology of the Modern World.* New York: Plenum Press.

Orser, Charles E., Jr. 1998. "The Archaeology of the African Diaspora." *Annual Review of Anthropology* 27: 63-82.

Orser, Charles E., Jr. 2001. "Race and the Archaeology of Identity in the Modern World." In *Race and the Archaeology of Identity*, edited by Charles E. Orser Jr., 1-13. Salt Lake City: University of Utah Press.

Orser, Charles E., Jr. 2007. *The Archaeology of Race and Racialization in Historic America*. Gainesville: University Press of Florida.

Orser, Charles E., Jr. 2023. *Historical Archaeology*. 3rd edition. New York: Routledge.

Parker, Susan R. 1997. "Men without God or King: Rural Settlers of East Florida, 1784-1790." *Florida Historical Quarterly* 69(2): 135-155.

Price, Richard, ed. 1996. *Maroon Societies: Rebel Slave Communities in the Americas*. 3rd edition. Baltimore: Johns Hopkins University Press.

Ramsey, William L. 2008. *The Yamasee War: A Study of Culture, Economy, and Conflict in the Colonial South*. Lincoln: University of Nebraska Press.

Rathbun, Ted A. 1987. "Health and Disease at a South Carolina Plantation: 1840-1870." *American Journal of Physical Anthropology* 74(2): 239-253.

Rediker, Marcus. 2007. *The Slave Ship: A Human History*. New York: Viking.

Reitz, Elizabeth J. 1979. "Spanish and British Colonial Subsistence Strategy at St. Augustine, Florida and Frederica, Georgia." Ph.D. dissertation, University of Florida.

Reitz, Elizabeth J. 1994. "Archaeology of a Colonial Creole Community: Wolstenholme Towne." In *Historical Archaeology of the Chesapeake*, edited by Paul A. Shackel and Barbara J. Little, 57-72. Washington, D.C.: Smithsonian Institution Press.

Reitz, Elizabeth J., and Nicholas J. Honerkamp. 1983. "British Colonial Subsistence Strategy on the Southeastern Coastal Plain." *Historical Archaeology* 17(2): 4-26.

Rupert, Linda M. 2012. *Creolization and Contraband: Curaçao in the Early Modern Atlantic World.* Athens: University of Georgia Press.

Schwartz, Marie Jenkins. 2000. *Born in Bondage: Growing Up Enslaved in the Antebellum South.* Cambridge: Harvard University Press.

Scott, James C. 1990. *Domination and the Arts of Resistance: Hidden Transcripts.* New Haven: Yale University Press.

Seed, Patricia. 1995. *Ceremonies of Possession in Europe's Conquest of the New World, 1492-1640.* Cambridge: Cambridge University Press.

Singleton, Theresa A. 1985. *The Archaeology of Slavery and Plantation Life.* Orlando: Academic Press.

Singleton, Theresa A. 1999. "An Introduction to African-American Archaeology." In *"I, Too, Am America": Archaeological Studies of African-American Life,* edited by Theresa A. Singleton, 1-17. Charlottesville: University Press of Virginia.

Singleton, Theresa A., ed. 1999. *"I, Too, Am America": Archaeological Studies of African-American Life.* Charlottesville: University Press of Virginia.

Smallwood, Stephanie E. 2007. *Saltwater Slavery: A Middle Passage from Africa to American Diaspora.* Cambridge: Harvard University Press.

South, Stanley A. 1977. *Method and Theory in Historical Archaeology.* New York: Academic Press.

South, Stanley A. 2002. *Archaeology at Colonial Dorchester.* 2nd edition. Columbia: University of South Carolina Press.

Stahl, Ann Brower. 2001. *Making History in Banda: Anthropological Visions of Africa's Past.* Cambridge: Cambridge University Press.

Tannenbaum, Frank. 1946. *Slave and Citizen: The Negro in the Americas.* New York: Knopf.

TePaske, John Jay. 1964. *The Governorship of Spanish Florida, 1700-1763.* Durham: Duke University Press.

TePaske, John Jay. 1966. "The Fugitive Slave: Intercolonial Rivalry and Spanish Slave Policy, 1687-1764." In *Eighteenth-Century Florida and Its Borderlands*, edited by Samuel Proctor, 1-12. Gainesville: University Presses of Florida.

Thornton, John K. 1998. *Africa and Africans in the Making of the Atlantic World, 1400-1800*. 2nd edition. Cambridge: Cambridge University Press.

Turner, Lorenzo Dow. 1949. *Africanisms in the Gullah Dialect*. Chicago: University of Chicago Press.

Weber, David J. 1992. *The Spanish Frontier in North America*. New Haven: Yale University Press.

Webster, Jane. 2008. "The Zong in the Context of the Eighteenth-Century Slave Trade." *Journal of Legal History* 29(3): 285-298.

Webster, Jane. 2021. *The Slave Ship: Memory and the Origin of Modernity*. New Haven: Yale University Press.

Weik, Terrance. 1997. "The Archaeology of Maroon Societies in the Americas: Resistance, Cultural Continuity, and Transformation in the African Diaspora." *Historical Archaeology* 31(2): 81-92.

Weik, Terrance. 2012. *The Archaeology of Antislavery Resistance*. Gainesville: University Press of Florida.

Wood, Peter H. 1974. *Black Majority: Negroes in Colonial South Carolina from 1670 through the Stono Rebellion*. New York: W.W. Norton.

Worth, John E. 1998. *The Timucuan Chiefdoms of Spanish Florida*. 2 vols. Gainesville: University Press of Florida.

Worth, John E. 2013. "Spanish Colonial Archaeology in the Southeastern United States." In *The Oxford Handbook of North American Archaeology*, edited by Timothy R. Pauketat, 565-576. Oxford: Oxford University Press.

ABOUT THE AUTHOR

R Jay Driskill is a professional archaeologist and bestselling author who transforms ancient mysteries into captivating narratives that educate and entertain. With academic credentials from the University of Florida and extensive fieldwork experience, Driskill brings authentic archaeological expertise to every page.

Specializing in historically accurate fiction and immersive non-fiction, Driskill's works have earned praise for their meticulous research, vivid storytelling, and ability to make complex historical concepts accessible to modern readers. Each book combines rigorous scholarship with page-turning adventure, offering readers both entertainment and genuine insight into humanity's fascinating past.

Whether you're a history enthusiast, archaeology buff, or simply love a well-crafted story, R Jay Driskill delivers meticulously researched narratives that will keep you engaged from first page to last.

Start your journey through time today – explore the complete collection and discover why readers call these books "unputdownable."

Visit rjaydriskill.com for exclusive content and upcoming releases.